VIOLENCE, UTOPIA AND THE
KINGDOM OF GOD

This controversial book, with a preface by Jack Zipes, explores the presence of the fantastic in Biblical and related texts, and the influence of Biblical traditions on contemporary fantasy writing, cinema, music and art.

The contributors apply a variety of critical concepts and methods from the field of fantasy studies, including the theories of Tolkien and Todorov, to Biblical texts. They challenge theological suppositions regarding the texts which take refuge in science or historiography.

Violence, Utopia and the Kingdom of God presents a provocative and arresting new analysis of Biblical texts which draws on the most recent critical approaches to provide a unique study of the Biblical narrative.

Tina Pippin is associate Professor of Religious Studies at Agnes Scott College, Decatur, Georgia. She is the author of *Death and Desire: the Rhetoric of Gender in the Apocalypse of John* (1992) and co-author of *The Postmodern Bible*. **George Aichele** is Professor of Philosophy and Religion at Adrian College, Adrian, Michigan. He is the author of *Jesus Framed* (1996) and co-author of *The Postmodern Bible* (1995).

VIOLENCE, UTOPIA, AND THE KINGDOM OF GOD

Fantasy and Ideology in the Bible

Edited by Tina Pippin
and George Aichele

London and New York

First published 1998
by Routledge
11 New Fetter Lane, London EC4P 4EE

Simultaneously published in the USA and Canada
by Routledge
29 West 35th Street, New York, NY 10001

Typeset in Garamond by Routledge
Printed and bound in Great Britain by Clays Ltd, St. Ives PLC

British Library Cataloguing in Publication Data
A catalogue record for this book is available from the British Library

Library of Congress Cataloguing in Publication Data
Violence, Utopia and the Kingdom of God: fantasy and ideology in
the Bible / edited by George Aichele and Tina Pippin.
Includes bibliographical references and index.
1. Bible as literature. 2. Fantastic literature – History and criticism.
3. Bible – criticism, interpretation, etc. 4. Fantasy – Religious
aspects. I. Aichele, George. II. Pippin, Tina.
B5535. V56   1998   97–49377
220.6'6–dc21   CIP

ISBN 0–415–15667–x (hbk)
ISBN 0–415–15668–8 (pbk)

CONTENTS

CONTENTS

CONTRIBUTORS

George Aichele is professor of religion and philosophy at Adrian College in Adrian, Michigan. He is the author of many articles on religion and fantasy and co-editor with Tina Pippin of two journal issues, *Semeia* and *The Journal of the Fantastic and the Arts* on "fantasy and the Bible." He is the author of *Jesus Framed* (1996).

Roland Boer is a lecturer at the United Theological College in Sydney, Australia. Among a wide range of interests, he likes to write books, the most recent of which is *Novel Histories: The Fiction of Biblical Criticism* (1997). He is at present at work on a volume on cultural criticism and the Hebrew Bible.

Jorunn Jacobsen Buckley, a historian of religions, specializes in the religions of late antiquity. Her main area is the religion of the Mandaeans, the last surviving gnostics from ancient times. For more than twenty years, she has taught in a number of academic institutions and is currently working at Massachusetts Institute of Technology.

Michel Desjardins is associate professor in the department of religion and culture, Wilfrid Laurier University, Waterloo, Ontario. Past president of the Eastern International Region of the American Academy of Religion (1991–2), and former American Academy of Religion/Lilly Teaching Fellow (1993–4), his publications include, *Sin in Valentinianism* (1990), *Peace, Violence and the New Testament* (1997), and *Whose Historical Jesus?* (1997), co-edited with W. Arnal.

Gene Doty teaches literature and writing at the University of Missouri-Rolla. His critical interests center around religion in fantasy and fantasy in religion. He is poetry editor for the

Webzine, *Recursive Angel* and has published his own poetry both on the Web and in hard copy. His books (published as Eugene Warren) include *Geometries of Light* (1981) and *Fishing at Easter* (1980). A collection of his ghazals is forthcoming from AHA Books on the World Wide Web.

William G. Doty is a professor of humanities at the University of Alabama/Tuscaloosa and Goodwin-Philpott Eminent Scholar in History, Auburn University, 1997–98. A prolific writer, translator, and editor, he has published seventeen books and over seventy essays in a wide range of journals. He is co-editor with Robert Detweiler of *The Daemonic Imagination: Biblical Text and Secular Story* (1990), and the author of *Myths of Masculinity* (1993) and *Mythography: The Study of Myths and Rituals* (1986). He edits *Mythosphere: A Journal of Image, Myth, and Symbol*.

Tina Pippin teaches in the department of religious studies at Agnes Scott College in Decatur, Georgia. She is a member with George Aichele of the Bible and Culture Collective, with whom she co-authored *The Postmodern Bible* (1995). She is the author of many articles on apocalyptic literature and culture, and a book, *Death and Desire: The Rhetoric of Gender in the Apocalypse of John* (1992) and a forthcoming book on apocalyptic bodies, with Routledge.

Eric S. Rabkin is professor of English language and literature and acting director of academic information processes in the information technology division of the University of Michigan, Ann Arbor. Rabkin has more than one-hundred-twenty publications, including twenty-nine books on such subjects as fantasy, science fiction, literary theory, and pedagogy. He has lectured widely to both general and academic audiences on those topics and on fairy tales, humor, US literature, culture studies, and administration.

Jack Zipes is professor of German at the University of Minnesota. He is a prolific writer and translator, a leading expert on the Brothers Grimm, and also a creative storyteller (especially of feminist fairy tales). He is the author of many articles and books, including *Fairy Tales and the Art of Subversion: The Classical Genre for Children and the Process of Civilization* (1986).

PREFACE

The spectacle and sacred nature of everyday fantasy and everyday violence

Jack Zipes

I write in the aftermath of the deaths of a fairy princess and a holy saint. Princess Diana and Mother Teresa died within a few days of each other in September 1997. Millions of people openly and dramatically expressed their grief and mourning. Their pictures along with many different images of Diana and Mother Teresa were beamed all over the world through television. The mass media carried all sorts of stories about the two, the fairy princess and the saint, so that little was left to the imagination. Fantastic spectacle was all that mattered.

We speculate with the fantastic. Spectacles violate our imaginations. The media and the corporate world seek to occupy our psyches and to manipulate our fantasies. Simultaneously, we project our fantasies onto reality and seek to occupy a space in which our most profound wishes and desires can be realized. In each instance—in the tension between corporate domination of the fantastic and individual projection of desire—we anchor our understanding of reality in the Bible and in fairy tales. Hence, Mother Theresa the saint. Diana the fairy-tale princess.

It is through fantasy that we have always sought to make sense of the world, not through reason. We have imagined gods, the kingdom of God, the miraculous feats of divine and semi-divine characters, and the commandments that have been established to lead us to the good life. It is through the fiction of our imaginations that we have sought to alter reality. This is why the Bible and certain fantasy literature are sacred texts: unlike reality, they open the mysteries of life and reveal ways in which we can maintain our integrity. They compensate for the constant violation of the sacred and the everyday violence in our lives that are engendered through spectacle.

It is a commonplace today that fiction, especially science fiction and fantasy, cannot keep pace with reality. Robots defeat world champions in chess. Animals are synthetically created, and all sorts of murderous experiments are conducted on animals. Space capsules circle Mars and Venus. Unbelievable scenes of ethnic cleansing and mass slaughter occur before our eyes in Europe and Africa. Cult suicides occur in Canada, Switzerland, and the USA because followers seek passage to another world. Throats of villagers are cut in Algeria in the name of Islam, while a writer by the name of Salmon Rushdie lives under a death threat because he allegedly wrote words insulting Islam. Political dictators like Pinochet and their torturers who mutilated and still mutilate thousands of people in Chile, Argentina, Iraq, and elsewhere continue to live comfortable if not luxurious lives. Tears can be detected from a statue of the Virgin Mary in Italy. My own in-laws have seen a UFO hover before their eyes on a summer evening in Wisconsin. Strange diseases that devastate large populations keep appearing throughout the world without apparent remedies in sight. Identical twins raised apart develop the same bizarre habits. Children are sold into prostitution throughout the world, or they are enticed by pornographers to perform licentious acts. Politicians and corporate heads tell blatant lies and deal daily in all forms of corruption in front of the public to pursue racist and sexist policies and to keep their power, while cries of "the emperor is wearing no clothes" go unheard.

We are all being surveyed and checked through amazing technology without our realizing it. Virtual reality mechanisms alter our sensory perceptions. Our everyday practices of work, buying food and clothes, attending school and college, and using objects in the household are conditioned by the spectacles of commercials and advertising that violate our inner and outer space.

Hermann Broch, the Austrian writer, who fled the Nazis, once asked, "Are we insane because we have not gone insane?". And this question is one to bear in mind when considering the Bible, fantasy, and violence. When the normal is so fantastically abnormal, what role can fantastic texts play in our lives? Can the violence in our everyday lives be more fantastic in literature and film? There is no simple answer here as can be seen in the compelling essays in the present volume edited by Tina Pippin and George Aichele. In fact, just as the function of the Bible as holy text has changed immensely in the last two thousand years, always dependent on the socio-cultural temper of the times, the very nature of fantasy itself has been transformed. In contrast to Tzvetan Todorov and Rosemary Jackson, who actually might have different notions of fantasy today after writing their seminal books in 1975 and 1981, I do not think we hesitate or are taken aback when we read fantasy literature. Today, for the moment, we turn to the Bible and fantasy literature for consolation, for a moment of calm, to reassess our values and direction. Consolation as expectation does not necessarily contradict Todorov and Jackson, but it does bring into question the nature of the uncanny and the unexpected in all fantasy literature. If nothing can be more uncanny, anxiety provoking, and incongruous than our everyday reality, then our turn to fantasy literature probably does not stem from our need for greater excitement and shock in our lives, but I want to suggest, for spiritual regeneration.

Reading fantasy literature is a retreat: a retreat from the alien-ating experiences in our lives. It is a challenging retreat to gather our forces, drives, hopes, and thoughts so that we can embark on an embattled voyage in everyday reality. Rarely do most people have time to read either the Bible or fantasy literature to reflect upon their lives. But when that time of reading comes, it is for a kind of spiritual regeneration and salvation. There is a religious intensity I have noted in devout readers of fantasy literature that says some-thing about the literature itself. This is not to say that all fantasy literature is religious or that reading fantasy literature will always be some kind of holy experience. In fact, most of what publishers (and the writers themselves) label fantasy literature is commercial kitsch filled with hackneyed motifs from ancient literature. Nevertheless, there is a quality of hope and faith in serious fantasy literature that offsets the mindless violence that we encounter in the spectacles of everyday life. If fantasy is subversive, then it wants to undermine what passes for normality, to expose the contradictions of civil society, to right the world out-of-joint in the name of humanity.

As fantasy, the Bible documents why violence and suffering occur in the name of God, and in this documentation, it proves (thank-fully) to be a faulty text. It shows itself to be all too human, and the disparate and contradictory voices of the Bible have given rise not simply to immense scholarly and religious commentary (a fantastic hermeneutical undertaking in itself), but to more fiction that weaves the motifs and themes of the Bible in pursuit of the same questions that the Bible raised and could not answer. Here I am thinking of Joseph Roth's *Job: The Story of a Simple Man* (1930). Written at the time when East European Jews still lived in impoverished *shtetls* and were threatened by pogroms, Roth sends a miserable and broken Russian Jew named Mendel Singer to New York, where a miracle restores a lost son to him. Then there is Archibald MacLeish's powerful drama *"J.B.": A Play in Verse* (1957), which turns biblical boils into atomic disaster in a modern setting. Or Mario Vargas Llosa's novel of magical realism, *The Storyteller* (1989), in which the branded Saul Zucatas joins a tribe of Amazonian Indians who represent to him a lost wandering Jewish tribe at the mercy of the violent force of civilization. We relate to Mendel Singer, J.B., and Saul Zucatas through the Bible and through the fantasy of their authors, who seek to provide solace from and in reality.

Job is but one strand of the Bible that enters fantasy literature because, like the myth of Sisyphus, it is a remarkable story about the absurdity and injustice of suffering, and it is also a testimony to the strength and courage of humankind. No matter how dark and sinister are those forces that violate our lives, we can discover our own human powers to resist such violence, without imitating the gods and the devils, and playing with other people's lives.

Today, for the moment, it is the resisting force of hope in fantasy literature and film that we need: the hope that we can realize some modicum of happiness by not succumbing to false gods and by refraining from exploiting other human beings for personal gain. Fantasy literature often explores biblical motifs and themes to provide a critical commentary on the Bible and to address the nature of evil and violence in our reality. The writers of the Bible coped imaginatively with the suffering and violence in their everyday lives and tried to project the possibilities for a more compassionate and humane world. Their heritage can be traced in fantasy literature, and it also informs the critical commitment of the authors in the present volume.

ACKNOWLEDGEMENTS

This book is divided into three parts; however, the overlaps and interweavings between the parts are probably more important than the differences between them. The articles vary considerably in style and content, as well as theoretical or methodological position. We do not attempt to be comprehensive or even fully representative here, either of biblical texts and themes or of interpretive approaches. Our collective focus is triple: on the biblical texts themselves, on fantasy theory and its place in literary theory and philosophy generally, and finally on the use of the previous two in analysis and critique of contemporary culture. Various of the contributions will balance these three foci in various ways.

The first part addresses the Hebrew Bible (the Jewish scriptures or Christian Old Testament). Eric Rabkin (English, University of Michigan) discusses the supernatural and cultural significance of forbidden food in biblical myth, traditional fairytales, and contemporary science fiction. Roland Boer (Hebrew Bible, United Theological College, Australia) compares the hallucinatory language and behavior of the prophet Ezekiel to the modern rock music star Axl Rose in terms of the interplay of anarchy and ecstasy, and how in each case self-destructive violence is contained by the dominant ideology of Western capitalism. Boer draws largely on interpretive categories provided by Mikhail Bakhtin and Antonio Gramsci. Tina Pippin (religion, Agnes Scott College) explores the controversial story in Genesis 6: 1–4 that concerns the creation of a race of giants resulting from the intercourse of the sons of God and the daughters of men. Pippin provides a feminist reading of several biblical stories of encounters with the alien and of the human desire to "know" the divine.

The book's second part focuses on the gospels of the New Testament. Jorunn Jacobsen Buckley (religion, Massachusetts

Institute of Technology) examines the relationship between Judas and Jesus in the gospel of John. The sadistic manipulation of Judas by both God and Satan becomes apparent in the language of the gospel, including particularly language about food and eating. George Aichele (religion/philosophy, Adrian College) explores the depiction of Jesus as a man of violence in the gospel of Mark's account of the cleansing of the Temple. The contest between Jesus and the Temple priests for the right to claim the kingdom of God is a "political" one, and Jesus' violent death at the hands of the true political lords, the Romans, is not unexpected.

The concluding part of the book raises larger questions about the Bible as a whole: questions of canon and Bible as the property of its various consistencies, questions of the overall meaning of the Bible and its relevance to humanity in the present day. Gene Doty (English, University of Missouri at Rolla) criticizes recent Christian fundamentalist and millenarian readings of the Bible that result in a sharp opposition between Good and Evil expressed in images of the blasphemous and the hideous. These understandings have so influenced contemporary US culture that they are often adopted unconsciously by non-fundamentalists as either typical of the Bible or even in entirely secular contexts. William Doty (religion, University of Alabama)—who is no relation to Gene—explores the "future-possible" dimension of fantasy and science fiction, that is, the possibility of exploring alternative futures that are possible is such fiction, not unlike Bloch's and Zipes's "anticipatory illumination." This same possibility appears in the eschatological and apocalyptic elements in the Bible, as well as the gnostic movement that was extremely influential during the early centuries of the common era and that produced many of the non-canonical writings of early Christianity. Michel Desjardins (religion, Wilfrid Laurier University, Canada) continues the reflection on gnosticism in relation to the writings of the late science fiction master, Philip K. Dick. Dick's own idiosyncratic views about religion and specifically the Bible serve both to introduce and criticize recent US religious paranoia.

We are very grateful to all of the scholars who have generously contributed essays to this collection. We owe a special debt to Jack Zipes (German, University of Minnesota) for his interest in and support for our work in this book and in others, and for his preface to this book.

INTRODUCTION

Fantasy and the Bible

Tina Pippin and George Aichele

The wolf shall dwell with the lamb,
and the leopard shall lie down with the kid,
and the calf and the lion and the fatling together,
and a little child shall lead them.
The cow and the bear shall feed;
their young shall lie down together;
and the lion shall eat straw like the ox.
The sucking child shall play over the hole of the asp,
and the weaned child shall put his hand on the adder's den.
They shall not hurt or destroy
in all my holy mountain;
for the earth shall be full of the knowledge of the LORD
as the waters cover the sea.

(Isaiah 11: 6–9 RSV)

These are they who have come out of the great tribulation; they have washed their robes and made them white in the blood of the Lamb. Therefore are they before the throne of God, and serve him day and night within his temple; and he who sits upon the throne will shelter them with his presence. They shall hunger no more, neither thirst any more; the sun shall not strike them, nor any scorching heat. For the Lamb in the midst of the throne will be their shepherd, and he will guide them to springs of living water; and God will wipe away every tear from their eyes.

(Revelation 7: 14–17 RSV)

The Bible is the seminal work of all fantasy literature.

(Zipes 1992: 7)

The lion and the calf shall lie down together but the calf won't get much sleep.

(Allen 1972: 28)

An interdisciplinary dialogue

The relation between religion and fantasy has been of central interest in fantasy studies for many years now. However, actual dialogue between fantasy theorists and biblical scholars and theologians is a relatively recent development. This dialogue draws upon methods from literary criticism, philosophy, comparative literature, biblical studies, and various other fields. It holds great promise for opening up new ways of thinking about the Bible in relation to fantastic literature and about the relationship of both biblical and secular fantasy literature to human experience. The present book is a collection of essays which seek to pursue this dialogue. These essays explore the presence of the fantastic in biblical and related texts such as the apocryphal and heretical writings, the patristic and early Rabbinic traditions, and also the influence of biblical texts, themes and traditions on contemporary fantasy writing, movies, music, and art.

We will not attempt to define the word "fantasy" at this point, for there are a variety of definitions current among fantasy theorists and several of them will be used in the essays presented here. We have no wish to impose a single definition on our contributors. We do caution the reader, however, that in this book we are talking about fantasy as a literary phenomenon, not fantasy as a psychological process, although literary fantasy and psychological fantasy are very likely related to each other. For example, Sigmund Freud's essay on "The 'Uncanny'" (1955) draws quite heavily on literary evidence, although its main interest is in psychological process. Both literary and psychological fantasy are very much concerned with questions of reality (see below). Nevertheless, while it is tempting to slide back and forth between literary and psychological views of fantasy, this would cause more confusion than understanding. A written text is not a person, and vice versa. Literary and psychological fantasy are distinct phenomena and are approached in distinctly different manners. The boundaries between the literary and the psychological are vague at times, but the primary focus of the essays in this book is on literature, that is, on written texts.

Another confusing vagueness that one runs into in fantasy theory concerns whether or not fantasy is a distinct literary genre. There is also a related terminological ambiguity regarding "fantasy" and "the fantastic." A genre is a type of writing, often but not necessarily thought of as a subcategory of narrative, such as comedy or tragedy, or more specifically, the melodrama, the thriller, the Western, and so forth. Each genre is defined by a set of codes which allow the reader to interpret the texts to which the genre is relevant. Correct identification of a text's genre enables the reader to form expectations regarding the meaning and the structure of the text ("they are falling in love," "the ending will be happy," "the hero has been brave," and so forth), and the further experience of reading this text is guided by fulfillment or frustration of these expectations.

In his important book on fantasy theory Tzvetan Todorov (1973) focuses on "the fantastic" as a particularly problematic area for any theory of genre. The fantastic, according to Todorov, lies in the reader's inability to decide whether a story belongs to one of two adjacent genres, the (natural) uncanny or the (supernatural) marvelous (1973: 25). Todorov argues that fantastic stories of this sort were produced only during a rather limited historical period, the late nineteenth and early twentieth centuries. In contrast, Eric Rabkin (1976) treats the fantastic as the reversal of the "ground rules" of reality, as we have learned to expect them, that occurs in stories of many different genres and time periods (1976: 9–10). According to Rabkin, when fantastic reversal becomes "exhaustively central" to a narrative, then the genre of fantasy emerges (1976: 28–9, 137). Thus there is a distinction to be made between the fantastic, as a narrative structure, and fantasy as a genre. Many scholars accept such a distinction between fantasy and the fantastic, even if they disagree with Rabkin in other areas.

Regardless of the definition of "fantasy," however, it is clear that literary fantasy and the fantastic (whether these two terms refer to one thing or to two distinct things) have a great deal to do with questions of theology and religion. How they are connected will vary depending on the definition of "fantasy" that is chosen. Rabkin's widely accepted view holds that fantasy (or the fantastic) involves the reversal of normal understandings of reality. In that case fantasy is, as J.R.R. Tolkien also argued, an act of "sub-creation" (Tolkien 1966: 49). The human power of subcreation is finally dependent upon our understanding of the reality of the "primary" or empirical world, even when we seek to deviate from that reality in the most striking ways. Tolkien defines the fairy story as a form of *evangelium*, the "good news" or gospel of human salvation and recreation (1966: 85–9). In other words, within a theological framework, human fantasy narratives imitate the creative power of God (Tolkien 1966: 75). This view is more than a little reminiscent of Samuel Taylor Coleridge's (1920) well-known description of the creative imagination as that aspect of the human spirit which is the image of God (although Coleridge assigned a lesser role to "fancy," his word for fantasy).

However, not all theorists accept this view of fantasy, as it implies in the last analysis an acceptance of "the way things are." Fantasy does not change oppressive reality, but rather fantasy delivers us from reality. In contrast, other theorists argue that fantasy is the power to subvert and overthrow established beliefs, in the cause of establishing a more just and humane world. Both Rosemary Jackson (1981) and Jack Zipes (1988) adopt such views. Jackson proposes that "[f]antasy re-combines and inverts the real, but it does not escape it: it exists in a parasitical or symbiotic relation to the real. The fantastic cannot exist independently of that 'real' world which it seems to find so frustratingly finite" (1981: 20). The fantastic story world remains dependent upon the primary reality of everyday life, but it does so in order to transform or invert that reality. This view understands the practical effects of fantasy differently than the preceding view: fantasy as revolutionary desire, not Tolkien's "consolation." However, in one important way the two views are quite similar: in both cases, primary reality is privileged, and fantasy or the fantastic takes the secondary position.

A more postmodern view of fantasy holds that the fantastic (or fantasy) is more indeterminate than either of these views suggests. In other words, humans cannot know reality at all apart from the medium of fantasy, and our understanding of reality emerges from our encounter with fantasy: the fantastic is prior to the real. Todorov argues that the generic indeterminacies of the fantastic interfere with the metaphysical beliefs which ground our sense of reality. The fantastic requires instead "near belief" (Todorov 1973: 31). The fantastic appears as a moment of indeterminacy between two different "realities," the uncanny and the marvelous. Thus for this view the question of genre and the question of reality are connected to each other. In its ambiguous relation to reality, fantasy raises profound metaphysical questions and challenges the reader's most solid beliefs. In this postmodern view the fantastic subverts not merely reality as we know it, but the very possibility of knowing reality. Fantasy provides neither consolation nor revolutionary certainty but a questioning of fundamental values and assumptions. The fantastic becomes a sort of anti-mythic, deconstructive power, threatening the coherence of the narrative, and the ambiguous and complex relation between fantasy and religion is highlighted, not resolved.

In some way, all of these views are correct. From the consoling and escapist tendencies of C.S. Lewis' Narnia books or Tolkien's own *Lord of the Rings* series, through the biting social critique in the works of Ursula Le Guin or Gabriel García Márquez, to the unsettling and paradoxical writings of Franz Kafka or Italo Calvino, many different types of story have been called "fantasy." This diversity is without doubt related to the unclarity regarding fantasy as a genre that we noted above, even apart from the confusing similarity to related genres such as science fiction or horror. Furthermore, various readers will often respond quite differently to the same fantasy story. This is particularly clear in relation to biblical stories: for example, is the book of Daniel simple pie-in-the-sky escapism or a call to arms? Or is it something else entirely?

Violence, utopia, and the kingdom of God

Our goal in this book is both to demonstrate the application of concepts and methods such as those of Tolkien, Jackson, Todorov, or Zipes (as well as many others) in fantasy studies to biblical texts, but also to open the Bible as a tremendous source text for understanding the fantastic. In particular the focus of each article in this book will be on elements of the fantastic in both the ideology of readers and the utopian language and imagery of the biblical narratives and other related texts. Does the Bible envision the kingdom of God as a site of violence? Do the reader's beliefs commit violence against the kingdom of God as a narrative element? It is our thesis that approaching the Bible by way of fantasy theory is particularly illuminating of this feature of the stories.

In the contemporary world we are familiar with images of the kingdom of God that are in large part drawn from the Bible. We understand the kingdom of God in terms suggested by the "peaceable kingdom" of Isaiah 11, the blissful salvation of the holy ones described in Revelation 7 (see the epigraphs above), or other similar images from biblical texts. We often think of the kingdom of God as a place or state of beauty, happiness, and profound personal fulfillment. The kingdom is an "other" world, whose connection to our present world of misery, ugliness, and disappointment is mysterious—never wholly certain except to the faithful, and never very far from the thoughts of even the most secular or least religious person. These images of the kingdom of God are so deeply woven into the fabric of our culture that they move and inspire us regardless of our religious views, or lack of them. We see and hear these images everywhere: not only in overtly religious contexts but in a wide variety of secular settings: magazine advertisements, popular movies and music, and many other places including ordinary, everyday conversations.

"The kingdom of God" as language in the Bible is associated with various images of salvation and justice, either in this world or some other one. As such the kingdom is a utopia, a "no place" (from the Greek, *ouk topos*). In our world today "utopia" has both negative and positive meanings. The negative meanings are the ones most often associated with the analyses of Karl Marx and Friedrich Engels: utopia as unreal pie in the sky, an opiate which both satisfies the oppressed and justifies the oppressor. For Marx and Engels, religion is particularly utopian, largely because of its fantastic notions of salvation beyond death. Likewise, many scholars and other readers view fantasy as an escape from the grim day-to-day realities of our "primary" world to the joys of a "secondary world" (Tolkien 1966: 60), in which good ultimately triumphs over evil through magic or other supernatural power. Tolkien indeed stresses the positive value of the escape and consolation provided by fairy stories. These stories are opiates, although Tolkien does not use that word. As anyone who has suffered prolonged and unavoidable pain can attest, opiates are sometimes necessary. However, no one would maintain that any person who requires an opiate is a healthy person. Fantasy is thus for this view a symptom of something very wrong with the primary world—perhaps one could say its "ungodliness."

The positive senses of the word "utopia" are often associated with the more recent, neo-Marxist view of utopia as "the principle of hope." For this view the "liberating magic" of fantastic stories "is not ethereal hocus pocus but the real symbolic potential of the tales to designate ways for creating what Ernst Bloch calls concrete utopias in the here and now" (Zipes 1984: xi). Fantasy does not merely console, but it also produces the "messianic power" to envision ways that the world could be better, and then to change it accordingly. Fantasy is not always equivalent to escape; fantasy can also and should also arise in the desire (or "anticipatory illumination") that leads to transforming action (Zipes 1992: 10ff.). This view also invokes the creative power of imagination, as suggested by Coleridge (1920).

It is not mere coincidence that these opposed understandings of utopia coincide with the first two understandings of fantasy described above. This should lead us to wonder what understanding of utopia would best fit the third, postmodern understanding of fantasy. Or is the postmodern upsetting of reality so profound that it admits no contrast between "no place" and "this place"?

Fantasy stories can be utopian in either positive or negative ways, and sometimes, it seems, the same story will be utopian in both ways at once! Many of the biblical stories, again, provide both status-quo-reinforcing comfort to some and revolutionary impetus to others. This difference in the reading of fantasy arises in part from the concrete situations of different readers, and in part from the interpretive preconceptions that are brought to bear on the text. It is here that the effects of ideology are most apparent: utopias are always profoundly ideological. An ideology calls for utopian images, in either their positive or their negative forms, and it manipulates them. In this way all ideologies are also theological—even the most atheistic ones.

By "ideology" we mean a set of beliefs and related practices which are implicated in the construction of the human world. Ideology reproduces images of the kingdom of God for various purposes. The essays in this book seek to uncover the effects of ideology on reading by exploring the other side (the under side, as it were) of the contemporary popular images of the kingdom of God: what the images leave unsaid, what they omit or distort, and so forth. It is here, we submit, that violence and utopia come face to face. Violence can be the physical violence of rape and murder, or it can be the mental or spiritual violence caused by hatred or oppression. In the Bible it also often takes the form of verbal violence, language which disfigures, dehumanizes, or erases altogether the human as object and as subject.

The prophets of ancient Israel and Judah condemn the human faithlessness and injustice that lead to divine wrath and doom for the nation, and John of Patmos dreams of an apocalyptic cataclysm in which powers of evil both human and superhuman are defeated and utterly destroyed by yet other supernatural powers. The price of the utopian kingdom of God is violence, and it is not only the violence of those who oppose the ways of God, that is, God's enemies. God also is violent, as are those who obey God. Indeed it is the violence attributed directly to God, as well as the violence of humans in obedience to God's will, that is most troubling about the biblical images of the kingdom. What do these images of violence, both natural and supernatural, human and divine, imply regarding the kingdom of God? What do they imply about the texts of the Bible, and about the ideologies that inform the Bible's readers?

1

EAT AND GROW STRONG: THE SUPER-NATURAL POWER OF FORBIDDEN FRUIT[1]

Eric S. Rabkin

A mythic dilemma

The notion of forbidden fruit lies at the center of the founding myth of Western civilization.

> Of Man's First Disobedience, and the Fruit,
> Of that Forbidden Tree, whose mortal taste,
> Brought Death into the World, and all our woe,
> With loss of Eden, till one greater Man,
> Restore us, and regain the blissful Seat,
> Sing Heav'nly Muse.
>
> (Milton 1667–74 [1962: 5])

"As [also] might have been expected," we read in *The Golden Bough* (Frazer 1922 [1969]), "the superstitions of the savage cluster thick about the subject of food; and he abstains from eating many animals and plants, wholesome enough in themselves, which for one reason or another he fancies would prove dangerous or fatal to the eater." Included in Frazer's world of examples is the report that "The head chief of the Masai may eat nothing but milk, honey, and the roasted livers of goats; for if he partook of any other food he would lose his power of soothsaying and of compounding charms" (Frazer 1922 [1969: 277]). It is difficult for us to disbelieve Frazer on this point because to our minds both soothsaying and charm making, on the one hand, and food taboos, on the other, are equally real and equally activated only within their shared social matrix. It would seem, in other words, that forbidding food is a crucial social act designed to sustain those who heed the interdiction. But contrary to Milton and Frazer, my thesis is simply that the act of forbidding food, while indeed a radically social act, is one designed not to sustain the hearer but rather the speaker. And narrative after narrative, from Genesis to the present, confirms this. Even before Milton mentions the fruit, he mentions "Disobedience." The control of food belongs to the strong; access to food is access to strength; and those who dare to violate the taboo, time and again, grow strong.

Milton, of course, would object that Adam and Eve, by their "mortal taste/Brought Death into the World," but, perhaps surprisingly, the biblical text does not support Milton. True, we read that "the Lord God commanded the man, saying Of every tree of the garden thou mayest freely eat: But of the tree of the knowledge of good and evil, thou shalt not eat of it: for in the day that thou eatest thereof thou shalt surely die" (Genesis 2: 16–17),[2] but Adam eats and does not die. He lives to be expelled from the garden, lives to till the soil, lives to sire Cain and Abel and, at the age of "one hundred and thirty years . . . begat a son in his own likeness, after his image; and called his name Seth: and the days of Adam after he had begotten Seth were eight hundred years: and . . . all the days that Adam lived were nine hundred thirty years: and he died" (Genesis 5: 3–5). Now, one can argue, of course, that had Adam not eaten the apple, he would not have died at all, but the text suggests otherwise, for when God discovers that Adam and Eve have eaten the forbidden fruit of knowledge, "the Lord God said, Behold, the man is become as one of us, to know good and evil: and now, lest he put forth his hand, and take also of the tree of life, and eat, and live for ever: Therefore the Lord God sent him forth from the garden of Eden, to till the ground from whence he was taken. So he drove out the man; and he placed at the east of the garden of Eden Cherubims, and a flaming sword which turned every way, to keep the way of the tree of life" (Genesis 3: 22–4). In other words, God did not visit Adam with death but rather prevented him from seizing eternal life. Mortality was humanity's original condition. That Adam the mortal lived nine hundred and thirty years and founded our species must not have seemed so circumscribed a fate to those tribespeople who first recorded the tale. And we cannot help but note that God is correct in seeing Adam as like Him, for just as God created Adam "in our image" (Genesis 1: 26), so Adam created Seth. In other words, the conflict in Eden, the primal disobedience, is between an older and younger generation of males. Against this father, Adam merely asserted his growing independence.

Perhaps this is why Freud wrote that "God is nothing other than an exalted father" (Freud 1950: 147).

I am always a bit reluctant to adduce Freud because so many of his followers, and sometimes Freud himself, have made claims that seem to me simply insupportable. In *Totem and Taboo* (1950), for example, he grounds all civilization in one stupendous crime. As Freud would have it, the primal horde of envious brothers was eager to have sexual access to their mother, so they killed their "violent primal father" and, "[c]annibal savages that they were, it goes without saying that they devoured their victim as well as killing him" (1950: 142). Freud recognizes that one need not believe in the historical reality of this consumption of forbidden food—"the mere existence of a wishful phantasy of killing and devouring him would have been enough to produce the moral reaction that created totemism and taboo" (1950: 160)—but, unfortunately, Freud reads the evidence of his contemporary anthropology as demonstrating "that primitive men actually did what all the evidence shows that they intended to do" so that "'in the beginning was the Deed'" (1950: 161). But even if we deny the Deed, we may well accept the Word. To forbid some foods and acts and to bid others seems a necessary, almost defining, behavior of human parenthood.

Lorenz (1966) has demonstrated that all vertebrates manifest intraspecific aggressive drives. While this is clearly proadaptive in partitioning feeding ranges and available mates according to the likelihood of reproductive success, this would be maladaptive were there no mechanisms to inhibit aggression against the young. If we reacted to a befouled baby as we would to a befouled dinner guest, the baby would soon find itself out of doors and beyond the nurturance of the adult community; in short, the next generation would die. We are, however, genetically programmed to soften at the sight of tears and to handle miniatures with care. And so we do not throw out the child who vomits on us; we do not take back the housekey from the child who lies; and we do not denounce to the police the child who steals. We keep it all "in the family." But keeping it in—repressing it in Freud's terms—does not obviate our aggressive feelings. Even in the most amicable of households, the parent at some points will fear that the child wants to cross the street or wander in the woods at too early an age and the child at some points will feel restrained by a parent perceived as exercising arbitrary power. In this sense, intergenerational conflict is biologically inevitable. Equally inevitable in this clash of congenitally aggressive wills is a tension that foresees the ultimate supplanting of the older generation by the younger, with,

typically, the attendant sadness and anger of the older and the attendant triumph and guilt of the younger.

In the growth of a human being, the onset of sexual potency is a
universal crux, a dividing line between the time of necessary childhood and the time of possible adulthood. Nothing so much seems to
demonstrate that one is no longer a biological child as the fostering of
a biological child of one's own. Adam, like God, creates Seth in his
own image. As we reach this crux, our own biology typically urges us
towards our genetic complements, males towards females and females
towards males, for without these complements we cannot produce
those biological children our bodies are being urged to create. Hence,
access to this complement symbolizes the actualization of our new
sense of potency, of power. Put another way, the inevitable conflict
between the generations will nearly always show itself symbolically
(even if not also literally) as a conflict over access to the sexual
complement as a sex object. Freud, ignoring women and taking the
symbolic for the literal, opines that "[i]t may be that we were all
destined to direct our first sexual impulses toward our mothers, and
our first impulses of hatred and violence toward our fathers; our
dreams convince us that we were" (1938: 308). I do not agree with
Freud in seeing what he calls the Oedipus Complex as fundamentally
grounded in actual sexual competition. But I do believe that the
language of sexuality presents us with uniquely resonant symbols for
discussing the inevitable conflict over the passage of power in all its
forms from one generation to the next. In order to distinguish this
general notion from the specific Freudian notion of literal sexual
conflict, we need another name. I propose the Eden Complex.

The Eden Complex

Lévi-Strauss has already shown that in a structural sense all versions of
the Oedipus myth may be seen as equivalent. Leach (1961) has shown
that the story of the Fall incarnates this same structure. Put most
simply, the main character (Oedipus and Adam) is young but
growing. He has an encounter with an older male (Laius and Elohim
[a plural male noun in Hebrew]) who tells him not to do something
(continue on the road or eat the fruit). The main character violates the
interdiction and winds up assuming the power of the older male
(ruling Thebes and creating in his own image). In both cases, the
dramatic substitution is symbolized by the young male having access
to a female who had previously been protected by the older male
(Jocasta as Laius' wife and Eve as presexual before the knowledge

brought on by eating the apple). As Sophocles, and, I suspect, Freud, would view it, this structure necessarily generates tragedy, but this need not be so. If the female is the wife of the older male, as is the case in *Oedipus Rex*, then of course the younger male is violating the social sanction of marriage (and also, as it happens, of incest). The outcome must either lead to a reversion to the *status quo ante* or the result will be some sort of tragedy, either the one we know from Sophocles or one in which the younger male fails in his contest with the older male and dies young and childless, as in *Hamlet*. On the other hand, if the female in question is a legitimate object of the younger male's desire, as is the case in *The Tempest*, then the outcome need not be tragic at all. Prospero sets Ferdinand the task of moving the forest in order to win Miranda and simultaneously demonstrate the younger man's recognition of the older man's authority. The play ends with Ferdinand and Miranda betrothed with the blessing of her father and the promise that when Prospero dies his natural death, Ferdinand and his children will succeed to the rule of Milan. Power, in other words, passes successfully between the generations. If we can call *Hamlet* an Oedipal tragedy, then we can call *The Tempest* an Oedipal romance. By using the term Eden Complex, I mean to indicate this basic triadic structure that supports the intergenerational conflict surrounding the transfer of power between characters of one sex and symbolizes their conflict by a struggle for access to a third character of the opposite sex. The Eden Complex, then, is different from the Oedipus Complex in having both Oedipal tragedy and Oedipal romance as possible outcomes and as being conceived as a fundamentally symbolic rather than literal sexual conflict.

Crucial in the story of Eden is the use of sight imagery. Freud, of course, took blindness to stand for castration, but I believe we can take it more generally as ignorance. Note that in all Indo-European words derived from the *gn* root and having to do with knowledge, intellectual and sexual knowledge are conflated (see Shipley 1984), as in the words "ignorance," "conception," "generate," "knowledge" itself, and, of course, "genesis." In biblical Hebrew, the same root that means "to see" means also "to perceive" and "to have sexual intercourse" (Gesenius 1829–32 [1964: 333b]). We have already mentioned in Genesis the crucial role played by creation in one's own "image." Eve is tempted by the serpent with these words: "Ye shall not surely die. For God doth know that in the day ye eat thereof, then your eyes shall be opened, and ye shall be as gods, knowing good and evil. And when the woman saw that the tree was good for food, and that it was pleasant to the eyes, and a tree to be desired to make one wise, she took of the fruit thereof, and did eat, and gave also unto her husband with her; and he did eat. And the eyes of them both were opened, and they knew that they were naked; and they sewed fig leaves together, and made themselves aprons" (Genesis 3: 4–7). The serpent tells the truth, it seems. He is a small voice within Eve asking her to use her own eyes. She does, and eating the forbidden fruit reveals something: shameful nakedness. This knowledge through the eyes, this revelation, is clearly both good and bad.

In *The Psychoanalysis of Fire* (1964b), Bachelard writes of four different congeries of meanings for fire. He calls each of these a complex, using that word in the sense that the parts are complected together. In "The Prometheus Complex," for example, we find "those tendencies which impel us to know as much as our fathers, more than our fathers, as much as our teachers, more than our teachers" (1964b: 12). The knowledge that equals may give us power, while the knowledge that exceeds may set loose havoc in the world. Think here of the fire that drives the darkness from the hearth and the fire that consumes the home. We see both in the DeLacey cottage at the center of Shelley's *Frankenstein, or The Modern Prometheus* (1818 [1969]). "The Prometheus Complex," Bachelard continues, "is the Oedipus Complex of the life of the intellect." Unlike Freud, and like both science fiction and the literature of Judeo-Christian revelation, Bachelard sees this complex as having both positive and negative possibilities. The whole point of Bachelard's complexes is that they represent conflicting potentials. When Moses asks to see God's face, he is told that "there shall no man see me, and live" (Exodus 33: 20), but Moses is able to survive seeing God's back. When Saul sees the light on the road to Damascus, he nearly loses his self; he is blinded and is restored only through divine intercession, arising with a new identity and a new name. The imagery of overwhelming light is standard in both Old and New Testaments, and everywhere that light represents good knowledge, it may also represent loss of self; everywhere that it represents new power, it may also represent death. The fruit looked desirable; they knew their nakedness. No matter which part of the antinomy is manifest at any given point in the text, the whole of a Bachelardian Complex is simultaneously potential as part of the symbol system of our culture. In delineating the Eden Complex, I mean to suggest not only its triadic character structure with the potentially tragic or romantic outcomes but also the thematic interest in intellectual and sexual knowledge and the imagery of light and sight, where knowledge and this light imagery may have both potentially good and bad outcomes.

Eden across the genres

An example of a work that demonstrates the Eden Complex is "Rapunzel". This story begins with a woman, one of a married couple who had "long wished for a child" (Grimm1812–22 [1886: 72]), seeing rampion ("rapunzel" in German) in the garden of the witch next door. The sight drives the woman to a frenzy and so her husband clambers over and retrieves some rampion. On a second trip, he is seen by the witch who demands to know why he is stealing. The rampion, then, is the forbidden food. He recounts his wife's craving and, without a word being said about sexuality, the witch says that "If it is all as you say you may have as much rampion as you like, on one condition—the child that will come into the world must be given to me." Like all myths, and like all true oral folk tales, the underlying issues are understood automatically by all concerned. This story abounds with both sexual symbolism and sight symbolism. When Rapunzel reaches twelve years old, the witch "shut her up in a tower in the midst of a wood, and it had neither steps nor door, only a small window above" (Grimm1812–22 [1886: 73]). We have the famous enactment of letting one's hair down, and when the witch learns that a man has climbed up to the girl, she abandons Rapunzel "in a waste and desert place" (Grimm1812–22 [1886: 74]). Then, mimicking Rapunzel by letting down the now-shorn hair, the witch entices the prince up again but pushes him down. He falls onto briars the thorns of which put out his eyes. "Several years" (Grimm1812–22 [1886: 75]) later, the prince is wandering blindly through the world, subsisting on roots (rampion, perhaps?), when he stumbles upon Rapunzel. She puts his head in her lap, cries at his blindness, and her tears falling into his eyes restore his sight. She and the twins she had borne him then go "to his kingdom, where he was received with great joy, and there they lived long and happily."

"Rapunzel" is a much richer story than this précis makes clear, but even a synopsis demonstrates the Eden Complex in a number of ways. In order to understand the story's psychodynamics, one needs to recognize that Rapunzel and her mother function in complementary ways in relation to the witch. In the beginning of the story, the intergenerational conflict is between the witch and the wife. Both are presumably childless, but the wife has access to a husband, the very one who will risk his life for the rampion. Thus the younger woman, like Adam, is able to manifest fertility but at some cost, here of the child itself. This is too great a price, and actually represents a displacement of gratification, for Rapunzel's mother drops out of the story and is replaced by Rapunzel. In the second half, the conflict is between an even younger wife, Rapunzel, who again has access to a man, and the witch. As Rapunzel is now the appropriate age of twelve, she should receive a man. Although this constitutes a violation of the witch's rules, after enough time passes, all is restored, and Rapunzel and the prince go off, not only fertile with their twins but to a much higher social position than Rapunzel's mother occupied. In short, just as in Genesis, the eating of forbidden fruit strengthens the character, and as in the Eden Complex generally, power (in this case both female fertility and social status) pass from one generation to the next. This is an Oedipal romance.

One can see an Oedipal tragedy in another version of "Rapunzel," Hawthorne's "Rappaccini's Daughter" (1966). Here the older generation character is split into Rappaccini, who has experimented mercilessly on his daughter Beatrice, raising her in a poisoned garden as a "human sister of those vegetable ones" he has made so deadly that ordinary people cannot approach them "without a mask" (1966: 116), and Baglioni, his scientific competitor. Seeing Beatrice from his own tower room that overlooks the garden, a young student named Giovanni is smitten with her, woos her, and eventually offers her a potent elixir to counteract the poisonous nature her father has instilled in her. But that is her nature, as she knows, and so, only to please Giovanni—and free him—she drinks it and dies. Baglioni, instead of feeling grief for a young woman he has known all her life, remonstrates: "Her father . . . was not restrained by natural affection from offering up his child in this horrible manner as the victim of his insane zeal for science. . . . Rappaccini, with what he calls the interest of science before his eyes, will hesitate at nothing" (1966: 133). Here we have the inversion of the garden of Eden, a garden of evil; in the place of the forbidden fruit we have the bidden elixir; in the place of the onset of fertility or some other knowledge and strength, we have death; instead of power passing from one generation to another, the older generation is made childless. Again we have an intergenerational conflict over power that relies on sight imagery reflecting knowledge in both senses.

It is not surprising that the garden itself is so frequent a part of works manifesting the Eden Complex. If the garden surrounds Adam the man, Adam is within the garden; it is the natural field for his own fertility. Consider the etymologies. In English we speak of the garden of Eden. "Garden" comes from an Indo-European root (*gher* IV; Shipley 1984) meaning enclosure and is cognate with "girdle." "Paradise," another word for the garden of Eden, comes from the

Persian (Shipley 1984: 64) meaning a garden with clay walls built up around it. The Hebrew word for garden, "gan," means a place protected by a fence, and comes to be used metaphorically for a chaste woman (Gesenius 1829–32 [1964: 13–14]), as in, "A garden enclosed is my sister, my spouse; a spring shut up, a fountain sealed" (Canticles 4: 12). And "Eden" means "pleasure" or "delight" (Gesenius 1829–32 [1964:608–9]). Hence, the biblical *gan eden* is an enclosure of delight, a woman set to receive a man. Here in this garden, as is natural once one reaches a certain age, the man looks towards a woman, that is, towards the fruit, for the very word "fruit" comes from an Indo-European root (*bhrud*; Shipley 1984) meaning "to enjoy." We still have this meaning in such phrases as "enjoy the fruits of one's labors" and "hard work bears fruit," and in the legal term "usufruct," meaning "the right to enjoy the use of something without diminishing it in value" (*Oxford English Dictionary*). As an English verb, fruit formerly meant, as it still does in the Spanish *disfrutar*, both "to enjoy" and "to make use of" (*Oxford English Dictionary*). *Gan eden*, then, is the enclosure of delight, the enclosure of the fruit, and if Adam is truly given the garden to use, the forbidding of a certain fruit is an attempt to thwart his very nature, for the nature of people is to delight in delight, to take pleasure in pleasure. But God does try to thwart Adam; God is frugal with the garden. "Frugal," like "fruit," comes to English through the Latin *frux*. "Frugal," of course, means to making sparing use of something (*Oxford English Dictionary*), while one of the forms of *frux* means "to improve oneself" (Simpson 1987). Just as Rapunzel "improves herself" socially by passing from childhood to womanhood and bearing "the fruit of her loins," so Adam, like God, should be able to create in his own image if only he has access to the forbidden fruit. The garden of pleasure, then, is a place where one may outgrow one's parent, or where one may die of parental restrictions.

In the Grimm brothers' fairy tales, there are many stories that use the Eden Complex and demonstrate that the consumption of forbidden fruit ultimately strengthens the one who violates the interdiction. "Hansel and Grethel," for example, are plagued by a stepmother who would have them, like Oedipus, exposed in the wilderness to die. Unable to return home, they spy the famous cottage of delicacies and are enticed within by a witch. Max Lüthi has pointed out that in true folk tales no one ever says "I love you"; instead, they give food. If the true marks of a mother are procreation and sustenance, that is, the desire to give life and food, then the true marks of a witch are infertility and cannibalism, the desire to kill and eat 1970: 111]). Hansel and Grethel meet a true witch who wants to fatten Hansel and consume him, but Grethel guards him. Finally, the deception failing, the witch says she will have him as he is. Grethel feigns inability to light the oven and when the witch leans in to start the fire, Grethel shoves her all the way in and roasts her. Releasing Hansel, they find their way home and discover that their stepmother is dead. Now that is convenient.

Psychologically, although Grethel does not actually eat the witch, she cooks her as if she were to be eaten, a murderous act now made licit by the threat against Hansel's life. The bidden food of the house has trapped the children; the forbidden food of the parent surrogate strengthens them. They not only escape but find their way home and find that their domestic problem has been removed. Why, one may ask, was there a domestic problem at all? As I have argued elsewhere (Rabkin 1979: 31–2), one may read the received story as the audible part of a longer story, one in which Grethel desires to supplant her true mother. When that mother dies, Grethel, of course, feels some guilt, and she is punished by the advent of the stepmother. At this point, the audible story begins. While one may not kill the father's wife, that is, the stepmother, one may kill a witch. Clearly the killing of the witch has made licit the imaginative act that Grethel had previously conceived as illicit. Recall that this story is set not in the house but in the truck garden where the father toils with the step-mother, in the forest, and again in the garden. Note the significance of bidden food as entrapping but the preparation of forbidden food as liberating. This follows the Eden Complex exactly.

In a variation combining "Rapunzel" and "Hansel and Grethel," one might observe that Cinderella through the good offices of her fairy godmother and by tending the hearth ultimately rises in social status above her own mother. Where, one might ask, does the fairy godmother come from? Again, one can imagine the tale as the audible part of a longer narrative, one that begins with the dispatching of the mother whose spirit returns as the fairy. Who dispatched the mother? In one Greek version, as Xanthakou recounts in *Cendrillon et les soeurs cannibales* (1988), the answer is clear. We will return to cannibalism later.

One might suggest that many of the Grimm brothers' tales are clearly not aboriginal narratives but at best Christian adaptations. No matter how one supposes the story of "Rapunzel" may have first arisen in vegetation worship, those eye-pricking briars are simply too reminiscent of Jesus' crown of thorns to seem completely sponta-neous. Perhaps so. But consider "The White Snake," one of the most obviously un-Christian stories in the collection. Here a servant each day brings a wise old king a special dish, a white snake, which no one save the king may eat. One day the servant steals some of the snake, eats it, and discovers that it confers the power to understand the speech of animals. Rather than being punished for violating the king's interdiction, the servant simply leaves, uses his powers intelligently and, ultimately, marries a princess and becomes a king in his own right. To see this story as within the Judeo-Christian tradition is to acknowledge that within that tradition, the consumption of forbidden food actually strengthens the consumer.

An enormous number of science fiction works use a highly ramified and specifiable version of the Eden Complex. Although it is not appropriate to elaborate on this notion here, I can say that this particular congeries, like "Rappaccini's Daughter," is characterized by our triadic character structure, our thematic interest in the passage of power between the generations, the imagery of knowledge and sight as both sexual and intellectual, the setting of the garden, the centrality of an isolated character who would be god or god-like, an aesthetic resonance with fairy tales (including bold colors and the indulgence of the Freudian notions of the illusion of central position and the omnipotence of thought),[3] and a dyadic system of value-laden images such as head/heart, male/female, master/slave, intellect/emotion, machine/spirit, and so on. Within these works, once one recognizes that the Eden Complex is at work, our knowledge of the pattern makes understanding of the whole very clear, just as in a Bachelardian Complex the recognition of one part suggests the active potential of all parts. To point only to two works, in Lewis Shiner's *Deserted Cities of the Heart* (1988), for example, once one sees that the grove of sacred, poison mushrooms contains the forbidden fruit, that the search for enlightenment is an attempt at god-likeness, that the ignorance of sexuality represents a stage before consuming the mushrooms, and so on, it becomes clear that once the hero does consume the mushrooms he will not only bring sexuality back into the world but will be cast out of the mushroom garden and begin a new world order. And so it happens—on a cosmic scale. In Sheila Finch's *Triad* (1986), once one realizes that Omareemee is a garden world maintained by a forbidding god-like race, that the motherly computer's prohibition against the native fruit is based on thinking of the humans as child-like, and that the search for heterosexual union underlies the character relations, it becomes clear that the pattern will work itself out in a consumption of the fruit leading to a new world order with a new kind of sexuality and increased mental

powers. And so it does. These works are both Oedipal romances fully
within the tradition of the Eden Complex. Plank (1968) has
suggested that *The Tempest* is the archetypal science fiction story,
primarily on the basis of Prospero as magician/scientist and what
Plank sees as the inversion of the Oedipus Complex.[4] I would rather
see *The Tempest* not as an archetype but as a prototype, revealing all the
elements of the full blown Eden Complex. Equally science fictional,
however, are the rarer Oedipal tragedies, like *Dr Faustus* and
Frankenstein, that do not offer forbidden fruit from which to draw
strength.

From literature to culture

We have so far discussed forbidden fruit within myth, fairy tale, and
science fiction. Another way to approach the subject would be
through the agency of interdiction. The foods we have considered
either were forbidden by the gods above us (the tree of knowledge),
were protected by the society around us (human flesh), or were obvi-
ated by the biology that constitutes us (poison mushrooms). Yet all
these prohibited foods gave strength to those who would consume
them. No matter what the agency, then, in narrative, rebellion pays.

As I mentioned earlier, Freud based part of his social reasoning on
the anthropological evidence for cannibalism. In many works, as
Huntington (1982) notes of early H.G. Wells, "cannibalism is a test
of difference: if cannibalism or the fear of cannibalism is involved (as
with the Morlocks and the Eloi [of *The Time Machine*]), then the two
species are really one, but if it is not involved, then they are separate"
(1982: 61). (Notice, by the way, that since cannibalism does represent
eating forbidden food, and since the Eloi live in what the Time
Traveller takes to be a garden, we should not be at all surprised that
the Morlocks are doing very well, thank you.) Anthropologists, in
comparing "endocannibalism," the practice of consuming those who
are within one's group, with "exocannibalism," eating only those
from outside one's group, agree with Huntington: "Thus the
members of a Marquesan tribe were more than ordinarily kind and
considerate among themselves and viewed the eating of a tribe
member very much as we view cannibalism. . . . At the same time,
members of other tribes were eaten without a qualm" (Linton 1936:
238). Cannibalism as a test of difference, then, cuts two ways as it
were: it includes the possible victim in one's species but it excludes
the victim from one's tribe. Such cannibalism has been thought to be
quite widespread. Frazer explains that much of it is an attempt

through sympathetic magic to gain the powers associated with special features of human anatomy, and he gives a list two pages long of the good parts (1922 [1969: 576–7]). Unfortunately for Frazer, after an exhaustive search of all the world's reported cases of cannibalism, Arens found that "excluding survival conditions, I have been unable to uncover adequate documentation of cannibalism as a custom in any form for any society" (1979: 21). Apparently, cannibalism is always and only used as an index of difference: we who are not cannibals are better than those others who are. When cannibal food was eaten that should have been forbidden but was instead bidden, as in the myths of Atreus and of Philomela, it took the gods themselves to set things aright. Thus Swift's *A Modest Proposal* (1729 [1996]) should have been self-evidently ironic. As it stands, however, the satire certainly speaks as if the consumption of human flesh would profit all involved. Or had Swift simply turned on its head his Strabo, the ancient source of the notion that the Irish themselves were cannibals?

In fiction, a key variant of cannibalism is vampirism. This practice alone has spawned an enormous literature (Carter 1989), although fortunately very few practitioners. One need not think long to see the stake in the middle of the vampire's heart in the middle of his earth-filled coffin as an attempt to restore the Garden. His sucking of the forbidden food is clearly both his access to secret knowledge and his source of a strength that repels God's dictum of mortality. The triadic relationship here between the vampire, the one he or she sucks, and the fiancé of the victim leads to an Oedipal tragedy for whichever character, vampire or fiancé, is unsuccessful, and an Oedipal romance for the one who is successful. The only case I know in which vampirism is benign is in the children's book *Bunnicula* (Howe 1979) in which a vampire bunny sucks vegetables white, but this benignity reflects the fundamental lack of conflict here: bunnies are supposed to consume vegetables. But people are never supposed to suck each other's blood. That is a forbidden food from which the monster draws its hideous strength.

One sort of prohibition that would seem self-evident, despite the case of Shiner (1988), is that against poison. And yet, when put in a narrative frame, even the forbidding of poison—rather than the mere existence of poison—yields an opportunity for the violator to gain strength. On Swift's floating scientific island of Laputa, "the most ancient student of the Academy," the one most revered, was he who endeavored "to reduce human excrement to its original food, by separating the several parts, removing the tincture which it receives from the gall, making the odour exhale, and scumming off the saliva" (1726 [1960: 145–6]). Think how great he would be if he could live off it! And remember, as Lucretius argued at great length, one man's meat is another's poison (*c*.94–*c*.55 BC [1965: 150–1]) because we all have different material natures. According to Krafft-Ebing, whose case histories admittedly may be no more factual than those of canni-balism but are just as likely to reflect a widespread ideology, those who voluntarily consume feces rather than dying find thereby extraordinary sexual potency (1965: 123ff.). The assumption of phys-ical identity among ourselves, like the assumption of cannibalism among others, is more an ideological than an empirical observation. In *The Food of the Gods* (1904 [1934]), Wells tells the story of the discovery and dissemination of a food that causes a multiplication of growth six or seven times in each linear dimension. The little people, ordinary humans, do not want their world changed, and so they pass laws prohibiting the consumption of this food. Needless to say, consuming the forbidden food confers immense strength. What is less obvious is that, once the battle is joined between the giants and the little people, the little people accuse the giants of war crimes. Why? Because they are "firing shells filled with—poison." Poison? Yes, the Food of the Gods itself, which would, after all, end their way of life (1904 [1934: 796]).

One can define a way of life in part by ways of eating. Our emphases on table manners, table settings, separate dining rooms, and so on indicate how far food is in our culture from a mere matter of refueling (Linton 1936: 440–1). In many works of narra-tive, just as cannibalism is taken as a sign of bestial savagery, the voluntary restriction of the diet to vegetarianism is often taken as a sign of nobility, and sometimes of noble savagery. Frankenstein's monster subsists on chestnuts; Wells' Eloi are frugivorous; and the inhabitants of Bulwer-Lytton's subterranean utopia are all vegetar-ians. While there is nothing forbidden about meat in these environments, the characters voluntarily refrain from eating it. Yet we cannot help but notice that the monster's ultimate power resides in his willingness to kill; Wells' Eloi are virtual cattle and the narrator of *The Coming Race* (1871 [1989]) understands that the sexual pun in Bulwer-Lytton's title refers not only to the Vrilya's burgeoning population but to the "little death" they will inevitably visit on us. Although a vegetarian diet may seem to mark "an Eden before the Fall" (Finch 1986: 163), clearly the majority opinion holds for the necessity of meat. If sight and light symbolize intellect in the Eden Complex, then food symbolizes the body: and we are body too, creatures of meat. But to eat meat, of course, involves killing.

It may well be that Adam and Eve were frugivorous before the Fall. "Adam" comes from the Hebrew *adamah*, meaning "earth," and refers to the ruddy color of both clay and sunburned people. The prohibition of food was against a fruit, and Adam's wife is not named. But then with the Fall, Adam is told that he must till the earth for his food and only then "Adam called his wife's name Eve; because she was the mother of all living" (Genesis 3: 20). Many people assume that this means that "Eve" is Hebrew for "mother," but this is not so. "Eve" comes from *haya*, "to live," a word originally meaning "to breathe" (Gesenius 1829–32 [1964: 273]). Genesis is here making a distinction, I believe, between the breathless living of the vegetable world, the world of clay, of *adamah*, of the garden, and the breathy living of the animal world, the world of fruit, of *haya*, of Eden. The English word "animal" itself comes from the Indo-European *ane*, meaning "to breathe" (Shipley 1984).

As soon as Adam and Eve go to live "at the east of the garden of Eden" (Genesis 3: 24), "Adam knew Eve his wife; and she conceived, and bare Cain, and said I have gotten a man from the Lord. And she bare his brother Abel. And Abel was a keeper of sheep, but Cain was a tiller of the ground" (Genesis 4: 1–2). The older son, in other words, was a gift from God, and was associated with vegetable life, as was Adam. The younger son is not viewed as a gift, but he keeps sheep and his sacrifice of them, the first mention in the Bible of killing, finds "respect" (Genesis 4: 4) in God's eyes while Cain's vegetable offerings find none. If we view Abel's killing of animals as a violation of a voluntary noble prohibition, and especially if we take a Christian prefigurative view and see his sheep as symbolic of Jesus, then what we have here is again the strengthening of the violator, the success of he who will eat forbidden food. But Cain, learning killing from Abel and jealous of him, kills his brother. Like Adam after eating the fruit, Cain hides, and again God finds the miscreant. Just as Adam was demoted from "pleasure" to tilling, now Cain is told that the ground will not bear fruit for him, so we must assume he has moved on to meat eating. Cain understands that he has violated a crucial taboo and wails that any who see him will slay him, so God puts a mark on Cain to protect him. (Some even say that this prefigures the Wandering Jew who must live until the second coming, or the undying vampire who became undead through the commission of two mortal sins.) And Cain "went out from the presence of the Lord, and dwelt in the land of Nod, on the east of Eden" (Genesis 4: 16), again, like Adam.

In other words, Cain brings murder into the world, but in so doing he gains protection and a diet of previously forbidden food, meat. When Adam fell, history began; when Cain falls, the first city (Enoch, named for his son) is built and civilization begins. The strength of the people again is based on the consumption of forbidden food.

Having considered all this, we are now in a position to offer at least one reason why Jesus is that "greater Man" Milton (1667–74 [1962]) sought to redeem us from our primal disobedience. In the New Testament, Jesus, the new Adam, takes the place of Cain, the second Adam. Just as Cain is marked with God's protection, so is Jesus. Just as Cain is the object of popular revulsion, so is Jesus. Just as all would slay Cain, so would they slay Jesus. And like Cain, Jesus brings into our diet the consumption of a forbidden food in order to strengthen us. But the food that Jesus brings us is much more radically forbidden, and hence much more radically powerful. "And as they did eat, Jesus took bread, and blessed, and brake it, and gave to them, and said, 'Take, eat: this is my body.' And he took the cup, and when he had given thanks, he gave it to them: and they all drank of it. And he said unto them, 'This is my blood of the new testament, which is shed for many'" (Mark 14: 22–4). To this day, if we are to believe Pope Paul VI in the 1965 encyclical *Mysterium Fidei*, it is not "right to treat the mystery of transubstantiation without mentioning the marvelous change of the whole of the bread's substance into Christ's body and the whole of the wine's substance into his blood" (in Arens 1979: 161). What Cain accomplishes by murder, Jesus accomplishes by suicide: each makes it possible for us to gain our strength through the consumption of forbidden fruit. But while Cain leads us to the earthly city, Jesus leads us to the celestial city. And while Cain would make us butchers, Jesus would make us cannibals, commanding us all to gain supernatural power through the consumption of forbidden fruit.

Notes

1 This chapter was first published in the archives of the Internet discussion group IOUDAIOS-L. It has since been reprinted in Rabkin *et al.* (1996: 21–38). Used by permission, University of Georgia Press.
2 All translations of biblical texts are from the King James version.
3 See Rabkin (1980).
4 See Plank (chap. 6, 1968).

2

EZEKIEL'S AXL, OR
ANARCHISM AND ECSTASY

Roland Boer

Music is prophecy. Its styles and economic organization are
ahead of the rest of society because it explores, much faster
than material reality can, the entire range of possibilities in a
given code. It makes audible the new world that will gradu-
ally become visible, that will impose itself and regulate the
order of things; it is not only the image of things, but the
transcending of the everyday, the herald of the future. For
this reason musicians, even when officially recognized, are
dangerous, disturbing, and subversive; for this reason it is
impossible to separate their history from that of repression
and surveillance.

(Attali 1977: 11)

. . . and heavy metal had emerged as one of the coolest, most
critically respectable and most diverse of musical forms.

(Straw 1993: 381)

What if Axl Rose, temperamental singer from the heavy metal band
Guns n' Roses, and Ezekiel, eccentric prophet from the Hebrew
Bible, were to be compared with each other? The exploration of this
rather far-fetched proposal—that is, a comparison between Axl Rose
and Ezekiel, and the phenomena they represent (heavy metal and
prophecy)—is the burden of this chapter, in which I want to make use
of a number of theoretical currents, in particular the long tradition of
political anarchism, Bakhtin's notion of the carnivalesque, the study
of ecstatic or possession behavior among prophetic and shamanistic
figures, the Gramscian concept of hegemony, and Attali's study of the
possible revolutionary, utopian, functions of music. An underlying,
and perhaps ultimate, concern here—coming from the arena of polit-

ical activism—is the possibility and means of effective subversive practice, particularly for the religious left, in the asphyxiating world of late capitalism. In doing so I will consider both the nature of prophetic subversion in the biblical text and seek to make some contribution to the ongoing debate concerning the political effectiveness of rock music. In what follows I will focus on heavy metal in the first two sections, with a shift to prophecy in the third.

Axl and anarchism

I'm such a Victory or Death type of person.
(Axl Rose, interviewed by Bill Flanagan 1992)

It seems to me that a good deal of sense may be made by considering heavy metal (and then later prophecy) from the perspective of the long political tradition of anarchism. Etymologically, anarchism refers to the absence of any form of organized governance. A distinction may be made that follows the historical development of anarchism itself—between plans for the utopian state beyond the necessary revolution and the increasingly violent process of destroying the old before the new may be inaugurated—a distinction that is succinctly expressed in the terms utopia and violence. Earlier writers and activists devoted more attention to the political, economic and social forms of an anarchist state of existence. For example, William Godwin (1756–1826), credited with the first full statement of anarchist thought in his *Enquiry Concerning Political Justice* of 1793 (in Joll 1979: 16), argued for the indissoluble connection between justice and happiness in social formation, for the abolition of property, the eradication of evil and crime through education. In Charles Fourier's (1772–1837) ideal anarchist society, "Harmony," social forms and the natural world were adapted to human needs and reason was to dominate. The "phalansteries," autonomous social and political units without an over-arching state, operated on the principle of selfless cooperation. And then Proudhon, strongly influenced by Fourier's utopian socialist ideals, proposed the complete abolition of capitalism and the establishment of direct, negotiated exchange of produced goods, without property or government larger than the commune. Work lies at the heart of his system, being both a social necessity and moral virtue. Yet it is Kropotkin, also influenced by Fourier, who embodies all that is peaceful and generous about anarchism. He argued, especially in *Mutual Aid* (1902), for a scientific theory of anarchist development, in which the tendency of the natural world was towards greater cooperation, mutual aid and sympathy, all of which would be enabled by proper economic organization and a new system of morality, without obligation or sanction. Echoes of the prophetic utopia of the Hebrew Bible are everywhere in these visions.

The second dimension is the role of the revolution itself, indelibly stamped by the experience of the French revolution in 1789, but especially the period of the *sans-culottes* in the spring and summer of 1793. If Kropotkin is the epitome of gentle planning in anarchism, Mikhail Bakunin (1814–76) is most closely associated with the other great tradition of anarchism: the value of violence and terrorism in the revolutionary struggle. His reputation stands mainly on his continual revolutionary planning and activity throughout Europe, especially his final period in Switzerland (1867–76). Less energy was directed towards envisaging the nature of socio-economic life after the revolution, although freedom was predicated on a lawless, stateless society, and on the goodness and generosity of human beings. The principle of "propaganda by the deed" was often enacted by anarchists through assassinations, bombs and symbolic acts of destruction against social institutions and people in positions of power, especially in the period 1880–1914. The names of Vaillant (on 9 December, 1893 he hurled a bomb into the Chamber of Deputies in Paris), Ravachol (whose name gave us *ravacholiser*, to blow up, after he planted bombs targeted at judges who had sentenced workers after the 1891 Mayday demonstrations), and Emile Henry (who was executed after planting a bomb in a Paris station), made anarchism synonymous with violence, while in Chicago there was the Haymarket bomb of 1886 and the subsequent execution of four anarchists on slender evidence. (I will later return to the question of political violence.)

While the first strand of anarchism is reflected in contemporary literature such as that of Kim Stanley Robinson's *Mars* (1992–6) trilogy, it is the second strand that I want to associate with heavy metal groups such as Guns n' Roses. It may be argued that Guns n' Roses enact a long tradition of bohemian anarchism characteristic of artists and writers and going back at least to the great revolutionary painter Gustave Courbet (d. 1877), a contemporary of Proudhon. Courbet's ability to offend both government and church is reflected best in his painting "Return from the Conference", which depicted a group of priests returning drunk from a meeting, and which was bought by a devout Catholic and then destroyed (see Joll 1979: 148). Courbet himself was known for his ability to drink and his rough peasant habits.

Yet musicians have not been immune from such tendencies, whether members of orchestras and choirs or jazz musicians (Miles Davis comes to mind). In the realm of rock and roll proper the first great musical anarchist, if I may call him that, was Guitar Slim (born Eddie Jones), who rose to prominence in the early 1950s, but died in 1959 at thirty-two from bronchial pneumonia complicated by alcoholism and a chronic lack of adequate sleep and food (see Palmer 1991: 665–6). In the 1960s Jimi Hendrix succeeded Guitar Slim. In a comparably short career Hendrix epitomized all that was socially objectionable in rock music. The famous film clip of Hendrix performing *Wild Thing* depicts the shock even Hendrix's audience felt at the the sight of him simulating sex with his guitar which is then set alight, smashed in pieces and thrown at the audience. Numerous other examples might be given of socially transgressive behavior from rock musicians—Elvis Presley (to begin with [see Hill 1991: 681]), Jim Morrison and the Doors, the Rolling Stones, Johnny Rotten and the Sex Pistols (and then the whole punk phenomenon), Joy Division, Kurt Cobain and Nirvana and an endless number of other grunge bands, are a few of the more well-known—but I have chosen Guitar Slim and Jimi Hendrix since, with their use of the electric guitar, they may be identified as the forerunners of heavy metal.

Heavy metal[1] is agreed to have begun with the album *Led Zeppelin I* in 1968, with its "brash, raunchy and musically subversive arrangement" (Hinds 1992: 151). In this tradition Guns n' Roses appeared as the peak metal band, at least in terms of popularity, at the turn of the decade from the 1980s to the 1990s, especially with the double album *Use Your Illusion* (1991).[2] *Appetite for Destruction* released only four years earlier was the best-selling debut album in the history of rock. At the same time the band had a frenzied and violent reputation, openly flaunting alcohol and drug consumption, sexual exploits, and the right to behave as they please. This includes flying in the face of censorship moves (the Parents Music Resource Center [PMRC] objected to what they felt was the band's glorification of a degenerate lifestyle), so that their lyrics (typically the censor's target) use graphic language, mention sexual bondage and discipline, psychological derangement and the effects of drugs. All of this is of course quite conventional for rock musicians, especially heavy metal, but it also signifies the rejection of a cleaner 1980s in which mainstream bands seemed to eschew such practices, at least in public.

But there is also another dimension of the rock and roll persona that interests me here. Whether cultivated or not, the image of the temperamental rock musician is well played out by Axl Rose, long haired blond singer for Guns n' Roses and "rock n' roll's bad guy" (Rose 1992b). Noted for destructive rages, his fragility and "hair-trigger temper" (Neely 1992), Rose's antics have both delighted and dismayed fans, especially his proverbial lateness to concerts and sheer unpredictability, and generally annoyed critics and the press. He also has a reputation as a misogynist, racist and bigot (mostly from the *One in a Million* [1988] song—there is a concerted effort to overcome the image). "We're not afraid to go to excess with substances, sexually and everything. . . . When we started we wanted to be the coolest, sexiest, meanest, nastiest, loudest, funniest band. There was a group consciousness of rape, pillage, search, and destroy" (Axlbio.html 1997). The drinking and drug use are flaunted with fans: "many times drugs and alcohol—there's a technical term that they're called, emotional suppressants—are the only things that can help a person survive and get through and be able to deal with their pain" (Rose 1992a). (In the interviews there is an effort to put this in the past.) There are the physical fights with Motley Crüe and David Bowie, the clash with Kurt Cobain at the 1992 MTV music awards, with Metallica on tour in August 1992, the two fans crushed at the Monsters of Rock Festival, the racial clash with Living Color, and the riot at St Louis on 2 July 1991. Axl has been arrested on over twenty occasions at his home in Indiana, was arrested after the St Louis riot (17 July 1992, after returning from the European leg of the tour), in Los Angeles during the Motley Crüe tour, and has various arrests for attacking security guards in 1987, two arrests during the Aerosmith tour of 1988, and after an altercation with his neighbor in 1990. Also, at least six law suits await resolution, from a former spouse, girlfriends, St Louis Riverport's Performing Arts Center, and by fans for a no-show in Montreal. Like Jim Morrison, Rose also presents himself as a reflective, angst-ridden philosophical type, given to deeper thoughts about human existence or its end. "Well, as you can see, being a fucking psycho basket-case like me does have it's advantages" (Axlbio.html 1997).

It is usual to focus on the lyrics, and eventually I too will need to do this, but it is only a part of the total media presence. A significant marker of the nature of a rock band—and this applies just as much to heavy metal—is the graphical display on album covers. The Guns n' Roses coat of arms, if it may be called that, features two revolvers end to end, wrapped in roses, over the band's name in a gold circle. Outside the circle is a rich, red splash of blood that drips down the page. Variations include a snarling skull and a circle of barbed wire. Alternatively, the skulls, representing the five band members, appear superimposed on a cross, on the appropriately titled *Appetite for Destruction* album (1987). Indeed the band photographs on this album evoke more of the gritty street (as also *G n' R Lies* of 1988) and explicitly showcase their substance abuse. Yet it is the picture "Appetite for Destruction" by Robert Williams, upon which the title of the album is based (the picture's signature has 1978), that is the most shocking graphic item. A semi-naked woman lies on the sidewalk, propped up against a fence and interrupted in peddling Mr Mini-Mites (small robots) by a larger, half dressed, robot. The robot is interrupted in the act of rape by a monstrous demon blood hound, bedecked with knives, armor and a host of parasite skulls. The moment of recognition for the robot is already too late, although it is not clear whether the woman will be killed in the expected mêlée.

The graphics for Guns n' Roses albums fit quite snugly within the broad expectations of heavy metal albums, as any visit to a heavy metal specialist store will soon reveal (although at the same time such visits open up the subgeneric variety of metal music itself),[3] but in doing so they also signify the (gendered) violence of such music. Although there are some exceptions, the overbearing gender presence in metal music is male, even more so, apart from rap, than other types of contemporary music. Indeed, Simon Frith describes heavy metal bands as "cock rockers writ large" (Frith 1990: 422; see also Frith and McRobbie 1990, with some essentialist misgivings). This is of course reflective of, and at the same time one of the constructive features of, the class/gender base of metal fans and bands, which is white, young, male and working class[4] (see Rubey 1991: 879, 884). I do not want to say too much about violence at this point, since such discussions move too often into liberal hand-wringing, except to note the ubiquitous signals of violence in some features of the Guns n' Roses phenomenon: the band title, its coat of arms and graphics, and the copyright holder (Uzi Suicide).

However, what is interesting about the lyrics is that the violence that is foregrounded in the various symbols and graphical representations dissipates in the lyrics. Indeed, the subject matter ranges through life on the street, hopeless childhoods, persecution, "life's a shit," alcohol and drugs, psychological disturbance, Oedipal longing, "vanilla sex," bondage and discipline, jaded and often broken love, and then the rejection of women and telling the world to get stuffed. At times the lyrics rise beyond the stage of Oedipal revolt (see Rubey 1991: 879) to a significant level of self-critical reflection, such as *Bad Apples* (1991) and *Don't Damn Me* (1991), and political comment, as in *Paradise City* (1987), *Garden of Eden* (1991), *Civil War* (1991), and

Knockin' on Heaven's Door (1991, a Bob Dylan cover). In the last two violence itself is criticized. If anything, the violence becomes that which is experienced by the implied singer, and then by extension the implied listener—the covert violence of lived experience, of everyday life. The standard psychoanalytic move at this point is to suggest that this sort of violence, but more especially the introspective, self-inflicted violence, is internalized violence, turned in upon the self in the forms of alcohol, drug abuse, mental derangement, and troubled sexual relationships. At times this also takes the form of kicking against the traces, against the world.

It is, finally, the overall "appetite for destruction" that connects Guns n' Roses with anarchism, particularly its violent, revolutionary form which has an extremely negative assessment of present, capitalist society, and a desire to see its end. The sort of anarchism that is pertinent here is that which focuses on the gleeful destruction of whatever existing, oppressive, socio-economic and cultural system is dominant. It is not for nothing that the fan club for Guns n' Roses is named "Conspiracy Inc."

Similarly, much of the prophecy of Ezekiel focuses on the need for destruction, usually cast in terms of punishment for the wrongs of the people. Such destruction applies not only to those outside Judah (Ezekiel 25–32), but also to Judah itself, particularly in the prophecies of doom in chapters 1–24. For example, in chapters 6–7, there are prophecies on the devastation of Israel's mountains (Ezekiel 6: 1–14), and the oracle of the bitter day of the end of the land (Ezekiel 7: 1–27). Chapter 22, at the other end of this collection, has the three pieces on the city of blood (Ezekiel 22: 1–6), Israel in the smelting oven (Ezekiel 22: 17–22), and the depiction of the corruption of all classes in the land (Ezekiel 22: 23–31). The desire for destruction is coupled with an absolutely negative assessment of present society. In contrast to heavy metal, however, and closer to the anarchist tradition, Ezekiel has some notion of what the restored society may be like, although his vision of a new city and new temple is far from anarchist hopes.

Axl and his world

What I want to do, however, is elaborate on my discussion of anarchism and heavy metal by considering the work of Mikhail Bakhtin, particularly *Rabelais and His World* (1984), a study of the function of carnival in the feudal period and the way it informs Rabelais's work. (It is important to note that this move from the era of capitalism back into feudalism opens up the question of the different forms certain cultural practices take in different socio-economic periods.) At some length Bakhtin moves through Rabelais's novels *Pantagruel* and *Gargantua*, dealing not only with the novels themselves but also the immediate historical contexts (e.g. the drought of 1532 and its inscription in the novels [1984: 439, 340]). Bakhtin's work was produced in a period when the medieval practices of the carnival were beginning to fade before the steady and violent advance of capitalism. He traces in characteristic formalist fashion (something for which he was constantly under suspicion) the importance of laughter, the grotesque, the language of compliments and profane, scatological curses (drawn from the marketplace), and the integral relations between images of eating, drinking, defecation, urinating, beating, death, and birth—usually in absolute extremes of violence, gorging and bodily elimination (which also includes sneezing, sweating, blowing one's nose and so on). For example, Pantagruel's stomach trouble produces much urine, which then becomes a series of hot, therapeutic springs in France and Italy. He recovers when men armed with picks, shovels and baskets are lowered into his stomach in a copper globe which Pantagruel swallows like a pill. Their entry through his gaping jaws is connected both with swallowing and devouring, as well as stomach, womb and childbirth. Banqueting, death, destruction and hell also find echoes here, as do thirst, water, wine and urine: "The grotesque body has no façade, no impenetrable surface, neither has it any expressive features. It represents either the fertile depths or the convexities of procreation and conception. It swallows and generates, gives and takes" (1984: 339).

Dan Rubey has suggested that rap music is close to Bakhtin's carnival, particularly as it is participatory, free and open, oriented to the future and not the past, and in its reversal of social hierarchy. But the real edge of carnival is found in the "grotesque, the raucous laughter and abusive language of rap, the emphasis on lower bodily strata which is part of the carnival spirit" (1991: 889; on rap's social effrontery, see Light 1991 and Garofalo 1993: 245–7). While rap arises from and appeals to black youth, heavy metal's appeal is, as I noted earlier, largely with young white males. And many of the features of carnival may be found in heavy metal music. Most obviously there is what Bakhtin calls the "language of the market place," where the restrictions of polite, social speech give way before gleeful swearing, cursing and continual reference to bodily functions and sex. The most obvious Guns n' Roses piece is *Get in the Ring* (1991), a track with a significant portion of the lyrics spoken so that they may be understood. It may best be described as a rich linguistic curse directed at critics, exploiters and unbelievers: "You wanta antagonize me/Antagonize me motherfucker/Get in the ring motherfucker/And I'll kick your bitchy little ass/Punk." The most memorable is that which attacks Bob Guccione Jr, of *Spin* magazine: "What you pissed off cuz your Dad gets more pussy than you?/Fuck you/Suck my fuckin' dick"[5] (1991).

The whole idea of excess, which for Bakhtin is incorporated in the theme of the banquet, is embodied more in the publicly portrayed lifestyle of groups like Guns n' Roses. The enormous proportions of the food, drink, and swallowing that form part of the carnival scene—excess eating and drinking is "one of the most significant manifestations of the grotesque body" (Bakhtin 1984: 281)—may be compared with the excess of substance abuse by Guns n' Roses. The alcohol and drugs that are very much part of their complex image function as a parallel to carnivalesque feasting (the alcohol of course has a one-to-one correspondence).[6] The key here is that it is not so much an escape from the world but a celebratory consumption of and triumph over the world.

The body itself (and Bakhtin is an important contributor to the renewed interest in the body in postmodern criticism), especially as a grotesque form, plays a crucial role in both Bakhtin's work and in the imagery of Guns n' Roses (and other metal bands). Bodily parts are paraded forth in carnivalesque literature, often with a reference to genitals: bowels, genitals, buttocks, stomach, womb, mouth and nose are all interrelated (nose and mouth being standard transferred loci for penis and vagina). Much of the bodily imagery is in what Bakhtin calls the "material bodily lower stratum"—all the imagery has a downward push, as it were, to what is below the diaphragm. The grotesque body is one that is incomplete, it is not closed off from the external world, but is open to it: what are important are its "excrescences (sprouts, buds) and orifices, only that which leads beyond the body's limited space or into the body's depths" (Bakhtin 1984: 318). Not only is eating, drinking and elimination important, so also is copulation, pregnancy and dismemberment. Both the graphic display of Guns n' Roses and its lyrics are replete with this sort of representation of the body. Images of band members feature naked torsos (I counted fifteen from four CDs), tattooed arms, and a variety of stills from frenzied public performances. When the bodies are adorned, it is with the characteristic flowing clothes of heavy metal bands, a variety of hats and heavy chains. The transgendered effect of the clothes, as well as the permed hair, has a distinctly homoerotic

dimension to it. Especially on the *G n' R Lies* album, various members
of the band strike orgasmic poses (mouths open, eyes shut), and Slash
appears in a standard soft porn spread pose, substituting his penis
with a beer bottle (on the videos his guitar has this function). The
lyrics feature bodily parts, such as the tongue, lips, ears, face, knees,
feet and asses, blood, shit, breasts, female genitals, usually as "cunt"
or "pussy," and also "flaps," and male genitals, although only as
"dicks." And then there are skeletons, dead animal bodies, dismem-
bered body parts, sex, death, and the grotesque body itself. The
grotesque body features heavily in Ezekiel's text as well, particularly
in the pornographic sections of chapters 16 and 23 and the grotesque
image of the flesh returning to the bones in chapter 37.

What interests Bakhtin is the systematic inversion that the
carnival provides: where misfortune is directed into celebration and
the powerful abdicate for a period of time. This is particularly the case
with the church, its festivals and its clergy. Each of the Christian
feasts had their carnivalesque parodies and the hierarchy of the church
found itself debased and mocked. The king becomes a clown and the
clown takes on the trappings of power. Debasement often moved
beyond verbal abuse to beatings and other violence, but it is a
violence that is beyond the ordinary, an extreme violence that is both
destructive and regenerative (the connections with anarchism should
not be missed). The mockery and laughter which was very much a
part of this extended to the most sacred items of Christian belief and
practice—death and resurrection, Eucharist, sin and salvation, the
feasts of Christmas, Easter, corpus Christi and so on. The ultimate
function of all of this was to reinforce the strong hierarchical structure
of medieval society and the church through the restoration of existing
patterns after the carnival. That which was most sacrosanct was
precisely open to the grossest parody and mockery. While this may be
read as a mark of respect, it also opens up the possibility, as in anarchism, of the destruction of those same structures and their
transformation into something new. Thus battle becomes feast,
slaughter turns into banquet, the stake becomes a hearth.
"Bloodshed, dismemberment, burning, death, beatings, blows,
curses, and abuses—all these elements are steeped in 'merry time,'
time which kills and gives birth, which allows nothing old to be
perpetuated and never ceases to generate the new and the youthful"
(Bakhtin 1984: 211). It is at this point that I need to move beyond
Guns n' Roses for a few moments (although the positioning of Guns
n' Roses at the tame edge of heavy metal is important for my later
argument) to the core of heavy metal. For it is here, with the various

subgenres of heavy metal itself that we find the extreme debasement of features of the dominant ideological structures of late capitalist society. For instance, hardcore metal parades incest, necrophilia, pedophilia, and excremental sex (see Hinds 1992 for the importance of explicit sexual reference in heavy metal), while death metal celebrates the myriad forms of death and its implications. Religion remains a dominant feature of much heavy metal, focused most often around Christianity or its traditional religious other, the occult. Bands like Deicide and The Impaled Nazarene go to extreme lengths in their inversion of Christianity, while older bands like Black Sabbath, Led Zeppelin and The Cult traveled the worn road of Satanism (once again, see Hinds 1992 on this, and its roots in the blues). Indeed, many carnivalesque practices trace their origin to the pre-Christian paganism of Europe. On the other hand, Mortification, an Australian metal band, attempts a more positive assessment of Christianity.

Although the moment is not always clear in all forms of carnival practice or heavy metal—whose relations should now be clear—both provide a hint of another world, another side to the normal drudgery of life lived now. Less explicitly than fantasy, science fiction and utopian literature,[7] carnival in its very overturning of social conventions and structures provides a glimpse, through its anarchic destruction, of an alternative world. This is sometimes envisioned more explicitly, as in the image of Pantagruel's gaping jaws that I mentioned at the beginning of this section. At one stage in the story a certain Alcofribas journeys into Pantagruel's mouth, where he finds a completely unknown world, older than this one and replete with twenty-five kingdoms. At the same time, it is a world that inverts this one, with people paid for sleeping rather than work (see Bakhtin 1984: 337–8). This is an appropriate image of the function of carnival in Bakhtin's assessment: the marketplace festivals, in distinction from the official feasts of the church, "were the second life of the people, who for a time entered the utopian realm of community, freedom, equality, and abundance" (1984: 9). The carnival is then a utopian event, something that foreshadows an alternative possibility in the face of the misfortune and disaster of present existence. Here it intersects most closely with anarchism, for both anarchism and carnival have distinct moments of destructive violence and the shape of a new world to come that is already enacted in the midst of the overturning of the old. Heavy metal works best when it tries to touch this liminal edge which then enables a glimpse of a better world.

Ezekiel and ecstasy, or the prone position

The intersection of anarchism and Bakhtin's notion of the carnival provides, it seems to me, a usefully overlaid way to understand the social function of heavy metal (the primacy of the social being one of Marx's legacies for us). I now want to make a belated turn to the biblical text of Ezekiel, where anarchism and the carnival, violence and utopia, make their presence felt. This will be all the more treacherous in that there is a growing awareness that these texts project an implied author who is not only mentally disturbed, if not schizophrenic, but also distinctly misogynist. Yet it is here that some of the contacts between heavy metal and prophetic texts may be located.

Following David Shumway's (1991) suggestion that rock music should be understood as a cultural practice—comprising music, lyrics, scores, concerts, videos, performers, listeners, appearance, substance abuse and attitudes—I want to suggest that prophecy also is a cultural practice, that it is a combination of words, actions, attire, assumed experience, and social and political context that constitutes prophecy, rather than any one item alone. There is perhaps greater need to assert this about prophecy, since the great tendency is to equate the prophetic literary texts with prophecy.

But, is it possible to read Ezekiel in terms of anarchism and carnival (something I have done spasmodically until now)? The link comes via the more conventional notion of ecstasy, possession, or trance: an intermittent category for some time now in research on the prophets. From the anthropological study of shamans (a term that is interchangeable with medium, diviner, or intermediary; see Overholt 1989: 4) among indigenous peoples in various parts of the world, as well as from psychological studies of altered states of consciousness, it has been argued that the prophets of ancient Israel form part of this larger social phenomenon (for contrary positions see Westermann 1967: 62–3; Parker 1978).[8] The textual representation of their activities—ranting, dancing, absence of fatigue, nakedness, catatonia, aphasia, visions, dialogue with the deity—show distinct signs of being ecstatic activity. The texts seem to describe individuals who "stand outside" their normal selves, and it is at this moment that the divine is believed to make its presence felt. Perhaps the most important study is that of Robert Wilson, whose "Prophecy and Ecstasy: A Reexamination" (1979) (see also the second chapter on "Prophecy in modern societies" in Wilson's *Prophecy and Society in Ancient Israel* [1980]) served not only to pick up the threads from earlier studies but also established Israelite prophecy firmly in the context of ecstatic experience. In moving away from the obfuscation of theological categories to those of anthropology and sociology, Wilson found that anthropology uses ecstasy, or trance, to describe a type of behavior rather than divine–human communication, the claim to such communication taking the form of "possession" and "soul travel." The great value of Wilson's work is the emphasis on stereotypical behavior for those in states of ecstasy and possession. The complex interaction between individuals and their societies explains this behavior, which is controlled by and conforms to these expectations. Thomas Overholt (1986, 1989) has since carried on Wilson's project, providing an extremely wide basis for comparison between contemporary prophecy in many different societies, emphasizing not so much what is said but the social dynamic of such intermediaries.

The usual exhibits of such stereotypical ecstatic or possession behavior by prophets are texts like 1 Samuel 10: 5–7, in which Samuel predicts that the newly anointed Saul will fall into a prophetic frenzy (the Hithpa'el of *nb'* is used here). The reporting of the narrative event in 1 Samuel 10: 10–13 uses both the Niph'al and Hithpa'el of *nb'* with the very similar meanings of "to speak prophetically," "to be in prophetic ecstasy," or "behave as a prophet." Wilson argues that this is controlled, and thus acceptable, ecstatic behavior. 1 Samuel 10: 6 is perhaps one of the best descriptions: "Then the spirit of the Lord will possess you, and you will be in a prophetic frenzy along with them and be turned into a different person." By contrast, other appearances of the verb relating to Saul describe uncontrolled, and therefore socially unacceptable behavior. The first of these is in 1 Samuel 19: 18–24, in which the uncontrollable spirit possesses three groups of messengers before Saul is himself possessed. In this story Saul strips off his clothes and lies naked for a day and a night, falling into a frenzy under Samuel. The same verb (Hithpa'el) is used in 1 Samuel 18: 10 to describe Saul's activity when the "evil spirit of God" (*ruach 'elohîm ra'ah*) came upon him. Even in this limited sample, prophetic activity and utterance is encapsulated in the same verb, although its precise nature seems to be unpredictable. Wilson (1979) has argued that the Hithpa'el of *nb'* was used "to describe characteristic prophetic behavior" (1979: 336), although what was characteristic varied with time and place. It referred both to ecstatic or trance behavior and, increasingly, particular forms of speech, eventually becoming synonymous with the Niph'al (thus 1 Kings 22: 8, 10, 18, 20–3; Jeremiah 14: 14; 23: 13; 26: 20–3; 29: 24–8; Ezekiel 13: 17; 37: 10; 2 Chronicles 20: 37).

It is then interesting to note where the verb is used in the prophetic literature, where it is most heavily used in Jeremiah and Ezekiel. In Ezekiel 4: 7 (restricting my focus to those chapters that interest me here) the text reads (New Revised Standard Edition of the Bible [NRSV]): "You shall set your face towards the siege of Jerusalem, and with your arm bared you shall prophesy (*uᵉnibbe'ta*, Niph'al) against it." The ecstatic dimension of the verb, or rather the ecstatic associations with the material concerning Saul, often fade away in the so-called writing prophets for all sorts of interesting ideological reasons (often expressed in the grammatical reasons I noted earlier), not least of which is the attribution of "undesirable" elements to the rejected king and more theologically desirable dimensions to the writing "prophets." Yet the Niph'al here would seem to convey a similar conjunction of an ecstatic prophetic act along with the ecstatic word, especially when the context is considered. For here the narrative speaks of a distinctly ecstatic act or series of acts on the part of the prophet in the midst of which he is then commanded to prophesy. It is begging for interpretation in terms of ecstasy.

The episode in which the verb is used (Ezekiel 4: 1–15) is the one in which Ezekiel is instructed by Yahweh to make a model of Jerusalem: on a brick Jerusalem is to be portrayed, siegeworks (wall, ramp, camps, and battering rams) are then to be arrayed against the brick-as-Jerusalem, as well as an iron plate that is to be between the prophet and the model. This war game is then exacerbated by the command to Ezekiel to lie on his left side for 390 days (LXX has 190), in some sort of symbolism for the period in years of the punishment of Israel. On behalf of Judah, the prophet is instructed to lie on his right side for forty days. It is not clear whether he is to gather his starvation rations of multigrain bread and water before taking up the prone position or whether daily relief will be permitted in order to do so. The issue of bodily elimination is not dealt with, although the implications of a little over one year and two months of defecation are rather alarming.[9] The sheer discipline, discomfort, and endurance required for this sort of act is one that suggest the sustained trance of an ascetic (see Cooke 1936: 50).[10] In Ezekiel 5: 1–4 the instructions continue. In this case, Ezekiel is to shave his head and beard, weigh the results and divide them in three. One part is to be burnt (inside the city when the siege [the mock one?] is over), another struck with the sword around the city, and the last scattered in the wind. Yet not all is to be dispersed: from a small reserved portion, Ezekiel will take a few strands and burn them in "the fire" (*ha'eš*). In chapter 5 the text falls over itself to get to the "application" (Ezekiel 5: 5–17, compare

4: 16–17). Yet it is important to note a feature of both these narratives that is all too often neglected: they remain at the level of Yahweh's command; there is no point where Ezekiel is reported to have carried out the instructions. Through being frozen on the divine tongue, as it were, these words, as well as the dialogue over the dung between prophet and God (Ezekiel 4: 13–15), are formally analogous with the Merkebah vision—they are various modes (visual, oral and aural) of communication with the divine, a central feature of ecstatic experience. Thus, it is as instructions that they are ecstatic, as well as any enactment itself.

Both of these acts are closely related to each other through their status as instructions without narrative execution. If enacted, they would constitute controlled, and thus acceptable, ecstatic behavior.[11] Some other ecstatic acts appear in the vicinity of these chapters. Catatonia or aphasia, a common aspect of an ecstatic period, is mentioned in both Ezekiel 3: 15 and 3: 26. In the first case, the prophet sits stunned (*mašmîm*),[12] after the story of what has the marks of an ecstatic visit to the gods or the spirits and divinely powered air transport (Ezekiel 3: 12–15)—he is lifted up by the spirit (*ruach*), "in bitterness[13] in the heat of my spirit, the hand of the Lord being strong upon me" (Ezekiel 3: 14; Blenkinsopp reads this as a description of ecstasy [1990: 28]). This is the only incident (in the texts I am considering), that is reported directly, for when we encounter the second incident of catatonia it is once again in the form of instructions, given by the "spirit," which had "entered into" him (Ezekiel 3: 24: *wattabo'bî ruach*). Here he is told to lock himself in his house, be bound with cords, and his tongue will cleave (*'adbîq*, "I will make to cling") to the roof of his mouth so that he is speechless (Ezekiel 3: 25–6). Only when Yahweh opens his mouth will he be able to speak to the people, although when this is to happen has been a cause for some exegetical consternation (see Ezekiel 24: 25–7; 33: 21–2; see Wilson 1972). Indeed, this material in chapter 3 has the strongest claim to ecstatic activity (thus Cooke 1936: 47), including the story of the eating of the scroll in Ezekiel 3: 1–3[14] (see Eichrodt 1970: 64). Now that I have regressed to the beginning of the stretch of texts that interest me (Ezekiel 3–5), it is possible to situate the instructions of chapters 4 and 5, and this is none other than as the words of the spirit (*ruach*) responsible for the ecstatic events in chapter 3, the same one that enters the prophet in Ezekiel 3: 24 and begins giving instructions that do not cease until Ezekiel 5: 4.

All of this suggests that Ezekiel 3–5 may be understood in terms of ecstatic, or possession, activity. Indeed, Cooke (1936: 42) reads the effect of the "hand of Yahweh" (*yad Yhwh*) in Ezekiel 1: 3; 3: 14; 8: 1; Isaiah 8: 11 and 2 Kings 3: 15 as that of ecstasy. If I add, without elaboration, the Merkebah visions in Ezekiel 1 and 10 and the vision of its movement in 3: 12–13, then a narrative character who is subject to ecstatic states and perhaps madness (the two are often closely related in the shamans of various societies, as also with rock musicians)[15] comes through with reasonable clarity (see Cooke 1936: 48).

Yet I want not only to add the category of ecstasy to anarchy and carnival to provide a much broader way of analyzing both prophetic activity and heavy metal, but also to use the whole practice of ecstatic prophecy to move on to the next phase of my argument. Before doing so, I need to attach the ecstatic label to Axl Rose and the practice of heavy metal music itself. And of course the obvious way to do this is via the word "ecstasy," which denotes not only a state of altered consciousness and behavior, but also a designer drug very popular in the 1990s, so named for obvious reasons. Ecstatic states were and are most often induced through changes in bodily chemistry, either through certain types of deprivation—food and sleep are the most common—or through additional stimuli, most commonly in herbs, drugs or alcohol, but also as music and noise. I have already stressed the importance of alcohol and drugs in heavy metal subculture, although with a focus on anarchism and carnival. As a category, ecstasy joins this group with very little effort. A few other features reinforce the connections: violence, a strong dimension of both anarchism and carnival, shows its face in the prophetic oracles of doom and the regular evocation of violent destruction. Although all three share in the wild breach of conventional patterns of behavior, ecstasy and carnival draw more closely together in that ecstasy is often induced in carnivalesque moments: the shaman or prophet was expected to rave at the carnival. Finally, the ecstatic is also anarchistic and carnivalesque in its ability to give some glimpse of a better world, an alternative world to this one.

However, what I want to pick up from the study of ecstasy and extend to anarchism and carnival is the point emphasized by Wilson (1979) and Overholt (1986): prophetic ecstasy depends very much on proper social dynamics in order to work. The dichotomy between uncontrolled, wild, behavior and speech on the one hand, and social expectations and legitimation on the other, is the sort of dialectical issue that allows me to move into the more explicitly Marxist areas of ideology and socio-economics.

Hegemony and noise

I have already moved into the realm of what, following Antonio Gramsci (1971: 268, 328, 348, 365, 370, 376), is now called hegemony. To begin with, the problem may be set up as an opposition between subversive forces and the efforts by the ruling classes to maintain social control. This is of course the basis of the classic Marxist understanding of class structure and class conflict (not surprisingly, given Gramsci's central role in the Italian Communist Party). Yet, the further such a relation is pursued the more complex it becomes. One may see an echo in discussions of rock music that return time and again to the issue of the subversiveness of rock (e.g. DeCurtis 1991; Born 1993; Buxton 1990; Davies 1993; Grossberg 1984, 1990, 1993; Hill 1991; Sturma 1992; Ullestad 1987; and Chow 1993 for a Chinese perspective on the same theme),[16] although Regev (1994) has argued that this is but a step on the way to the traditional (Romantic) claim for the autonomy of rock music as an art form (see also Stratton 1983: 153). How may rock undermine social norms? My own chapter, coming as it does from a perspective similar to that of Gramsci, trades on this question, extending it to the role of prophets in the biblical text and in ancient Israel. And so, in a further turn of the original opposition, the question becomes how the anti-social and subversive behavior of the prophets, and so also metal groups such as Guns n' Roses, is in tension with the effort, by the very social forces they wish to undermine, to contain them. This might also be phrased in terms of the continual attempt to harness and redirect the disruptive dimensions of anarchism, carnival and ecstasy.

Hegemony is, then, the dominant ideological structure in a given society, the exercise of power without direct violence. The study of hegemony is concerned with the struggle of the ruling classes to set the ideological agenda for all social classes, attempting to structure desires, feelings, practices, expectations and thoughts. Yet this ideological control is never secure, never complete, and so there is a contradictory move both to allow discontent and a certain level of rebellion—in order to allow people to vent their feelings—and a continual effort at encirclement of those elements that are too subversive. At first sight there would seem to be little hope, as my closer look at the notion of ecstasy above suggests. The possibility and nature of ecstatic behavior is controlled by a whole range of unexpressed social expectations which serve to (de)legitimate the prophet or shaman in question, as emphasized repeatedly by Overholt (1986, 1989). Similarly, the behavioral patterns of Guns n' Roses and other heavy metal groups fall into expected anti-social patterns so that they may then be identified as precisely what they wish to be, a heavy metal group. This type of ideological control works at a couple of levels: first, there are the norms of marginal social groups or so-called "subcultures" which normally have strict codes of behavior.[17] Thus, Guns n' Roses conform in many respects to the codes of what may be described as the heavy metal subculture—their type of music, their "lifestyle," their substance abuse, in short, being repulsive to dominant middle class culture. What is significant about Guns n' Roses is that they form a rather mild and toothless type of heavy metal. There is a much stronger edge to groups like Ministry, Deicide and the Impaled Nazarene, and yet they themselves conform to the expectations of metal subculture as well. In a similar way prophetic texts such as Ezekiel operate on the basis of shock value: the sheer negativity of the judgment passages, the violence continually evoked as a divine prerogative, and the misogyny of many sections, to name a few examples.

The second level of hegemony over heavy metal and prophecy is in the wider social expectations of the behavior of such subcultures. It is as though, in a perverse way, a group like Guns n' Roses is expected to be involved in precisely the sorts of things in which they *are* involved. Yet, whenever these expectations are transgressed, the machinery of censorship is brought to bear. Similarly, there seems to be in the Hebrew Bible a symbiotic, although not exclusive, relation between prophecy and kingship: prophets played a political role that was either appreciated, tolerated, or repressed. Yet there was an expected way in which the cultural phenomenon of prophecy should operate.

There is, finally, a more comprehensive level of control in operation, for the controlling ideologies of a particular social formation are adept at incorporating and using for their own ends the strongest oppositional forces, either as neutralized forms of critical thinking or as negative examples to avoid. Thus prophets such as Ezekiel had their words recorded (assuming for a moment the existence of an Ezekiel) and eventually collected in a religious canon, and rock groups such as Guns n' Roses become what may be termed a "research arm" of multinational capitalism, setting patterns for clothing fashion, hair, physique, food and so on. Guns n' Roses is crucially positioned between the subversive core of heavy metal and its softened, commercial side, but the group also signals the always-already commodified nature of the most extreme forms of metal music. The most pervasive way rock music as a whole is incorporated into mainstream commercial culture is through advertising (the continual re-use of certain riffs and words on television advertisements), sports programs (here heavy metal functions as a background to masculine events) and in the video clips themselves, which may be understood as advertisements to buy the recording (see Herman 1993: 14). Similarly, the Hebrew prophets, even those like Ezekiel, who were the ideological heroes of the reformers, have become the texts of largely middle class, elderly and conservative churches, who practice a liberal, hand-wringing, approach to social justice that incorporates the prophets among their central texts.

But to speak of "incorporation" is to grant some external existence to a subversive current in prophecy and heavy metal, something that Grossberg (1984) terms "excorporation". Yet, as David Buxton has suggested, countercultural values are not always in conflict with commercial processes: "it is important not to see rock music as a perpetual conflict between two pure entities, counterculture and corporate capitalism, in which the latter always unfortunately appropriates the former to its own ends" (1990: 434). Buxton backs this up with an argument for the integral role of the star system, the burgeoning of the record industry, and the suggestion that recorded music has "become one of the key elements in the constitution of the modern self, increasingly defined in terms of lifestyle" (1990: 434). These arguments are in themselves elaborations of Adorno's classic argument in "On Popular Music" (1990), which, using the model of Tin Pan Alley music production, suggested that popular music is riven with the marks of capitalist production—standardization and pseudo-individualization. There is no chance here for any viable opposition from a mode of cultural production that is capitalist through and through, although Gendron (1986) has argued that Adorno's homologous connection between the production line and popular music is a little too simplistic.[18] Indeed, Guns n' Roses is itself now a corporation, with Axl and Duff the sole owners.

This is in the end a rather bleak prospect for any subversive and marginal practice, whether in prophecy or metal music, unless an alternative culture can be established in which these patterns of existence are nourished. While I am not in the habit of turning too quickly to the possibility of subversive practice, Gramsci's notion of hegemony has a second dimension, which is that the efforts at encirclement and control by the dominant ideological structures are never complete, hence the frenzy of such efforts and their sheer crassness (such as the national anthem at all major sports events). There are, it seems, shards of opposition that remain, or, to avoid the modernist perception of resistant enclaves, modes of opposition that have not yet

been explored with sufficient vigor, at times generated out of capitalism itself, as Dyer argues regarding disco (1990: 412). I also want
to avoid Grossberg's twist on the "enclave" argument, in which the
edge of rock and roll lies in its ability to create a "rupture between the
rock and roll audience (in their everyday lives) and the larger hegemonic context within which it necessarily exists" (Grossberg 1990:
116).[19]

In order to locate the possibility of viable opposition, and also to
move onto my conclusion, I turn to the remarkable work by Jacques
Attali, *Bruits* (Noise) (1977). For Attali (once economic adviser to
Mitterand in the early days of France's Socialist experiment), music is
the *"organisation du bruit"* (1977: 9), a remarkably prescient description, perhaps even a definition, of heavy metal itself. Working with
the conventional Marxist model of base and superstructure, Attali
takes not a retrospective approach, seeing the superstructure as
lagging behind and thereby dependent on, or determined by, the
base; rather, he investigates the possibility that the superstructure
may anticipate new social formations with which the base may in
time catch up. It is music that plays this annunciatory role for Attali,
foreshadowing in its own peculiar way the potential of another, better
mode of production, but also the possibility of a much worse state of
affairs, which is itself the underside of the promised improvement.
What is attractive about Attali's proposal is this ambiguity that he
traces in the promise of music. The very chance of a new social and
economic formation depends upon Attali's perception that the new
forms of social relations may be seen developing all around us, in the
cracks of the old as it begins to break up, and that the new economic
order that is part of these social relations is foreshadowed in cultural
production such as music, especially popular music. It takes little
extension to suggest that it is precisely those forms that operate on
the extreme edge of mainstream culture, such as heavy metal, that
may be said to provide, in their very anarchism and carnivalesque
practices, a taste of radically new social, political and economic
formations. Cultural forms such as music or prophecy may therefore
have profoundly utopian functions.

That this provides a Marxist model for understanding prophecy
hardly needs to be mentioned. Prophecy, then, like music (especially
heavy metal), provides glimpses as an item of the superstructure of
an alternative world that the economic base may one day realize. In
this thoroughly materialist way of approaching prophecy, what will
then be interesting is whether the modes of production that follow

that of the Hebrew Bible may be traced in the prophetic texts themselves.

However, I do not want to close without offering some comments on the role of violence in the utopian vision. My earlier discussions of anarchy and carnival indicate the crucial role of violence in both of those cultural and political practices, particularly in the need for the destruction of a present corrupt order before the new may be inaugurated. The problem of course is that in both heavy metal and so much of Ezekiel the violence is gendered violence, something that is of course as undesirable as racial or sexual violence. Yet, I want to suggest that these are examples of misdirected violence, of an explosion into unacceptable realms of what should be political violence, for the primal impulse of anarchism and carnival is precisely political violence. And this may, unfortunately, be required in the light of the implications of hegemony with violence, hegemony being the originary and usurping violence of a social structure whose violent character has been effaced. Indeed, as Žižek argues, the highest form of violence is that which coincides with the absence of violence, that is, this supreme violence "determines the 'specific colour' of the very horizon within which something is to be perceived as violence" (1994: 204). This framework then simultaneously conceals its originary violence while designating that which disrupts as violence. This of course means that hegemony, in its very concealment, is the location of supreme violence: any act of violence that disrupts and makes explicit *this* violence is what may be termed political violence. And this is where the daring suggestion of Jan Tarlin (1997) finds its place: he argues that in the very pornography (which he understands as the conjunction of sexual representation and violence) of Ezekiel's texts may be found a utopian glimpse that breaks the hegemonic shell. It is then a sad reflection on our own situation—and it seems of Ezekiel's texts—that the strength of the originary, hegemonic, violence requires something like Ezekiel or Axl Rose to offer the possibility that it may be broken.

Notes

1 I follow David Shumway (1991) in speaking of a "cultural practice." It is not exclusively records, lyrics, written music, videos, performers, listeners, clothes, appearance, attitudes—it is all of these things and more that come together to represent a way of life lived by those young people who choose to do so.

2 Dan Rubey (1991: 879) notes that heavy metal as such is the most popular music for MTV viewers.

3　My autobiographical insertion at this point is to identify my much loved local metal store—The Hammer House Metal Shop in Parramatta, Sydney, Australia.

4　In this respect it carries on the class connection of rock and roll itself (see Frith 1981).

5　The mix of heteroerotic and homoerotic imagery here is interesting in itself. See Garratt (1990: 402–3) on the ambiguous sexual construction of pop stars.

6　See especially the songs on *Appetite for Destruction* (1987).

7　On this see my *Novel Histories* (1997) with Sheffield Academic Press, especially chapter 4. See also Rosemary Jackson's *Fantasy: The Literature of Subversion* (1981).

8　Zimmerli, in a restrained manner, allows only "a strangeness of psychic experience" (1979: 17) by someone who "was overwhelmed by images and visions up to the point of actual physical emotional participation" (1979: 20), otherwise refusing to speak of ecstasy or possession, a refusal also found in Greenberg's (1983) commentary. Brownlee (1986), in a moment of breathless insight, mentions the effects of "trauma" (1986: 58), and an "internal-emotional" state that coincides with Yahweh's "internal-volitional" hand and the "physical" sensation of the "spirit-wind" (1986: 41).

9　Perhaps the command to use human dung on which to cook the food is intended to deal with this problem (4: 12).

10　Others have suggested a physical disease such as catalepsy or mental illness (see the discussions in Eichrodt 1970: 83–4 and Zimmerli 1979: 17–18).

11　Although it is the association with symbolic magic that has bothered more than one commentator (see, for example, Eichrodt 1970: 81).

12　Reading the more difficult Hifʿil participle of *šmm* instead of the often amended *meʿšōmem*, the easier polʿel participle

13　LXX has no comparable word for *mar*, prompting many commentators to omit it from translation. The sense remains the same: "in the [angry] heat of my spirit." See Zimmerli (1979: 94). Brownlee (1986: 36, 38) reads *rm* instead of *mr*, basing the amendment on the Hexaplaric *meteôros*, "in midair." So: "I soared aloft in the ecstasy of my spirit," yet Brownlee takes a low view of ecstasy.

14　Axl Rose also mentions that the Bible was "shoved down my throat, and it really distorted my point of view" (Rose 1992b). Cooke (1936: 37) relates 3: 1–3 to 2 Esdras 14: 38–41, where Ezra drinks a cup "full of something like water," but with "a color like fire" (verse 39) with the effect of increased understanding, wisdom and memory.

15　The interviews with Axl Rose indicate something of his troubled psyche (Rose 1992a).

16　On the other hand, De Curtis' McLuhanite analysis of rock music, with its strong technological determinism, leaves no room for any consideration of oppositional possibilities.

17　Straw (1993) argues against a heavy metal subculture, largely due to the suburban habitation of its audience, a situation that removes intermediary strata between groups and audiences that is needed to foster a subculture (club circuit, social marginality). Straw writes about the

1970s, and he admits the growth of such intermediary strata in the 1980s, including small-scale magazines, specialty stores and the paraphernalia of fandom.

18 See Peterson and Berger (1990) and Stratton (1983) for a further detailed study of the commercial business of rock music. The volume *Rock and Popular Music: Politics, Policies, Institutions* as a whole attests to the intricate ways in which rock music is part of the complex web of capitalist society and politics.

19 A later development of this (Grossberg 1993) is to speak of the contradictory patterns of the "mattering maps" that rock enables through its rhythms: a territorializing pattern is set over against deterritorializing "lines of flight" which place rock outside the mainstream of everyday life. Born (1993: 281–8) attempts to use "alterity" as a possible category for resistance.

3

THEY MIGHT BE GIANTS: GENESIS 6: 1–4 AND WOMEN'S ENCOUNTER WITH THE SUPERNATURAL

Tina Pippin

Introduction: divine intervention

Once upon a time in the Bible people lived amazingly long lives, animals talked, giants roamed the earth, God intervened on the battlefield, prophets healed and resurrected the dead, and women became pregnant by male deities. The border between the heavenly and earthly worlds was thin; God and sons (are they angels? other deities?) transgressed this border frequently. This story in Genesis 6: 1–4 is part of the miraculous universe of biblical stories, although many scholars (and readers) want to ignore this text or explain it away as being completely different from the rest of Genesis.

In this strange passage in Genesis 6 the sons of God see that the daughters of humans are fair, come to earth and take them as wives, and these women give birth to a super race of warriors. This story relates an earlier time when angelic beings roamed the earth and intermingled with humans. The intercourse of divine beings with human women is a common story in global mythologies. In this case of women giving birth to a race of giant men most of the focus is on the men (fathers, sons and grandfathers). I want to switch the focus to the women. Feminist fantasy and science fiction theorists would call this relationship an "interspecies marriage." I will be utilizing feminist readings of the fantastic as I trace the trail of this story in other biblical supernatural figures (e.g. Jacob fighting the angel, Goliath, Samson, other angelic beings), the Annunciation, through Talmudic interpretation, medieval Kabbalah (in one story a rabbi brings a

Frankenstein figure to life), and Jewish tales of the supernatural. The presence of alien, supernatural beings in the Bible has been over-looked by biblical scholars who want to label these beings under a single category, "the divine," which shifts focus from their alien status. Encounter with supernatural beings is one of the central themes in the Bible, and the context and details of these encounters are diverse. I want to show that this desire for a supernatural world with supernatural beings is a desire to return to a form of Eden and a desire to know the "divine" more intimately and share divine powers. What effect does this desire have on women? What is the effect of reading the Bible in terms of the supernatural?

God's pro-creation

The translation from the Parashas Bereishis reveals interesting details of this story in Genesis 6: 1–4:

> And it came to pass when Man began to increase upon the ground and daughters were born to them, the sons of the rulers saw that the daughters of man were good and they took themselves wives from whomever they chose. And Hashem said, "My spirit shall not contend evermore concerning Man since he is but flesh; his days shall be a hundred and twenty years."
>
> The Nephilim were on the earth in those days—and also afterward when the sons of the rulers would consort with the daughters of man, who would bear to them. They were the mighty who, from old, were men of devastation.
>
> (Scherman 1993: 27)

This translation is in juxtaposition with the garden of Eden story (death is brought into the world), the Noah story (120 years until the flood and mass devastation) and the Babel story (the men have a name which denotes arrogance). The Talmud notes that the initial phrase, "and it came to pass," always "presages trouble" (*Megillah* 10b) (Scherman 1993: 27, note 1). It is a signal of an ominous beginning; something bad is to follow. The usual translation, "when" (NRSV) or "now look" (Rosenberg 1990), denotes a more neutral beginning. This translation of the sons of God as "the sons of the rulers" (*elohim*) reflects an allegorical interpretation of the sons of Seth mating with the demonic daughters of the sons of Cain. The medieval rabbis and Augustine, Luther and Calvin preferred this interpretation. The note in the Parashas Bereishis on Genesis explains also that the sons of the rulers were a company of angels or celestial beings (which the LXX picks up translating sons as angels), since whenever *elohim* was mentioned there was the notion of rulership (Scherman 1993: 27, note 2). The medieval rabbis explain the narrative further: "The daughters of man were the general populace (R' Saadiah Gaon); the multitude, the lower classes (Rambam Moreh 1: 14), who did not have the power to resist their superiors (Radak). Thus, the Torah begins the narrative of the tragedy by speaking of the subjugation of the weak by the powerful" (Scherman 1993: 27, note 2). There is a subversive power to the story, for the heavenly realm is blamed for overextending its dominating power, even if the celestial beings made the daughters "wives."

Biblical scholars reveal the difficulty in navigating this supernatural story. This text has been called "an abbreviated myth," a "tale of emergence" and a "descent narration" by Susan Niditch (1985) and a *Schuld-Strafe* story and a "myth of organization" by David Peterson (1979: 49). Julius Wellhausen (1885) referred to the narrative as a "cracked erratic boulder" (1885: 317). Walter Brueggemann (1982) sees this text as marginal and even admits, "The narrative must not be pressed too far because we do not understand it" (1982: 72)(!). Niditch connects Genesis 3, 6: 1–4 and 11: 1–9 under the theme "ideal order to reality" (1985: 59–60). She notes that the latter two stories have no "negative value judgement" (1985: 38, 40) by themselves, only when they are connected in a larger theological agenda.

In *The Woman's Bible* (1990) this story is "a myth like those of Greek, Roman and Scandinavian fable, demi-gods love mortal maidens and their offspring are giants" (Blake 1990: 38). Josephus (*c.*37–*c.*100 CE) concurs that "the deeds that tradition ascribes to them resemble the audacious exploits told by the Greeks of the giants" (*Antiquities* I.73). Comparisons of Genesis 6: 1–4 with the Babylonian Atrahasis epic and other Near Eastern texts do not go very far, since there is no divine–human mating. There are really no historical roots to this story, as there are for the flood narrative. Variants of the story of the gods having sex with humans run throughout cultures.

Many scholars argue that this brief episode stands on its own as a narrative whole, while others argue it is an abbreviated Canaanite myth. Of the overall narrative structure Philip Davies (1993) states: "The author of Gen. 6: 1–4 has chosen to digest this story because left undigested, either outside or inside his own story, it would undermine, indeed it would oppose, that story" (1993: 198). Niditch echoes this sentiment in a different way: "The absorption of the divine makes mankind not more divine but more human" (1985: 38). In its present context this story is wedged into the flood story and is part of the wickedness that brought about God's wrath.

Translation variations lead to alternative weavings of this story into the whole of Genesis. In *The Book of J* (1990) poet David Rosenberg also offers an interesting translation:

> Now look: from the earthling's first step man has spread over the face of the earth. He has fathered many daughters. The sons of heaven came down to look at the daughters of men, alive to their loveliness, knowing any they pleased for wives.
>
> "My spirit will not watch man so long," Yahweh said. "He is mortal flesh." Now his days were numbered: to one hundred and twenty years.
>
> Now the race of giants: they were in the land then, from the time the sons of heaven entered the rooms of the daughters of men. Hero figures were born to them, men and women of mythic fame.
>
> (1990: 68–9)

Rosenberg and Bloom call J a woman of the David/Solomonic times who has a "humorous and subtle imagination" (1990: 34). Bloom says about J's attitude: "Since Yahweh is clearly male, and considerably less mature and sophisticated than the aristocratic ironist J, it is appropriate that his author handles him with a certain reserve" (1990: 34). The character of God is in question here, as it is for Jack Miles (1995) in his biography of God.

Miles distinguishes between the sons of Elohim (God) and the sons of Yahweh (the Lord), stating that the sons of Elohim (and not Yahweh) took the daughters of men: "And it is the Lord who objects to this coupling" (1995: 41). This is a strange distinction that the text does not make: how many creator deities are there in Genesis? Clearly Yahweh and Yahweh Elohim are one deity and Miles's interpretation causes a split in the heavenly head. A further question is: how many *procreative* deities are there in Genesis?

The Rosenberg translation attempts to reconstruct the narrative to include giant women as well as men among the Nephilim. Since the root of Nephilim is "fallen" or "fallen ones," this elevation of heroic giants at the end of the narrative makes the switch in Genesis 6: 5 even stranger; how could such heroes be the cause of God sending the flood? By contrast, the Talmudic notes edge the reader closer to the abyss; the "men of devastation" show us the watery chaos to come.

1 Enoch elaborates the story of the sons of God and the Nephilim and gives the story an apocalyptic spin. I Enoch 15: 3–12 describes the action of the divine beings:

> For what reason have you abandoned the high, holy, and eternal heaven; and slept with women and defiled yourselves with the daughters of the people, taking wives, acting like the children of the earth, and begetting giant sons? . . . But now the giants who are born from the (union of) the spirits and the flesh shall be called evil spirits upon the earth, because their dwelling shall be upon the earth and inside the earth. Evil spirits have come out of their bodies. Because from the day that they were created from the holy ones they became the Watchers; their first origin is the spiritual foundation. They will become evil upon the earth and shall be called evil spirits. The dwelling of the spiritual beings of heaven is heaven; but the dwelling of the spirits of the earth, which are born upon the earth, is in the earth. The spirits of the giants oppress each other; they will corrupt, fall, be excited, and fall upon the earth, and cause sorrow. They eat no food, nor become thirsty, nor find obstacles. And these spirits shall rise up against the children of the people and against the women, because they have proceeded forth (from them).
>
> (Isaac 1983: 1–22)

In 1 Enoch the women seduce the divine men and lead them astray (Book 19 [1983: 1–2]). Further, the women are unclean. There is a theme of pollution, and sin is once again connected with the women. "Go, bind Semjaza and his associates who have united themselves with women so as to have defiled themselves with them in all their uncleanness" (1 Enoch 10 [1983: 11–12]). The women know secrets from the angels, who taught them about the heavenly realm. A contemporary version of 1 Enoch is represented by the angels in the Wim Wenders's film, *Wings of Desire*; these angels survey the torn city of Berlin; they are watchers of the urban alienation of humans.

Who, then, is the hero of this story? According to Graves and Patai (1963), in one retelling of the myth "the sons of God were sent down to teach mankind truth and justice," which they did for three hundred years. Then "they lusted after mortal women and defiled themselves by sexual intercourse . . . before the end they were indiscriminately enjoying virgins, matrons, men and beasts" (1963: 100). Are these divine beings, heros or villains? The flood disaster is still present, if repressed. The only dialogue is by God, who basically states that he will not put up with humans anymore. Standing alone, the story could be hopeful. But, in its present position there is no chance of utopia or a happy ending. God is a destroyer; even giant offspring cannot escape the oncoming deluge. Who is the real monster in the flood story? Are the giants monstrous? Are the sons of God good or bad angels, or are they morally ambiguous? Which character is really violent in Genesis 1–11? God is the one who unleashes the violent flood. Georges Bataille gives the reason for God's actions:

> The Christian God is a highly organised and individual entity springing from the most destructive of feelings, that of continuity. Continuity is reached when boundaries are crossed. But the most constant characteristic of the impulse I have called transgression is to make order out of what is essentially chaos.
>
> (1986: 119)

When giants roamed the earth

The giants who roamed the earth in the old days were named Nephilim, but they were known by other names: "*Enim* ('Terrors'), *Repha'im* ('Weakeners'), *Gibborim* ('Giant Heroes'), *Zamzummim* ('Achievers'), *Anakim* ('Long-necked' or 'Wearers of Necklaces'), *Awwim* ('Devastators' or 'Serpents')" (Graves and Patai 1963: 106). The Gentile enemies were monstrous in proportion. The enemy loomed large; exaggerating body parts was part of making sense of the Other.

The root of Nephilim is from "*napal*, 'to fall,' hence probably 'the fallen ones'" who "exist only to die in a great destruction" (Hendel 1993: 556). The Midrash Rabbah (I refer to the Freedman and Simon edition 1939) has the following description: "*Nefilim* denotes that they hurled (*hippilu*) the world down, themselves fell (*naflu*) from the world, and filled the world with abortions (*nefilim*) through their immortality" (218). Hiwi al Balkhi (ninth century) believed the Nephilim built the Tower of Babel (Davidson 1967: 206). The Nephilim cracked the barriers of divine–human. Kathryn Hume notes that "in Genesis, this fantasy of special birth is projected at a national level, and the stories involving the supernatural are woven to confirm this identity" (1984: 115). Hume is referring more to the special births of the "legitimate" patriarchs, but the birth (or rather, appearance, since the text does not directly mention their birth) of the Nephilim is really "special." Possibly they could live forever, and their offspring could live forever (against Genesis 3), posing another danger to God's ultimate power, until God limits their life span.

Many scholars inject the story with a hypersexual reading. Gerhard von Rad (1972) sees the Nephilim as celestial beings of "the upper heavenly world" who "let themselves be enticed by the beauty of human women to grievous sin; they fall from their ranks and mix with them in wild licentiousness" (1972: 114). Von Rad reads a pornographic substory into Genesis 6. Robert Newman summarizes: "The Jewish view sees the 'sons of God' as judges or noblemen and the 'Nephilim' as violent warriors. The sin involved is unrestrained lust, rape, and bestiality. The Christian view sees . . . the sin as mixed marriage between the Sethites and the Cainites" (1984: 35). According to van Gemeren "Elsewhere angels may appear in human form, dressed as men, eat, drink, walk and are subject to being molested (Genesis 18: 1, 2, 8; 19: 1, 5). Here we are dealing with fallen angels who apparently have no regard for God" (1981: 346). Davies reads the text more closely to glean that "Sin begins in the heavenly world, in which no hint of enmity is present. . . . A disordered male heaven violates a female earth" (1993: 199). Because the story is so brief, the temptation to fill in the gaps is great. The text does not relate the details of the sin, but readers want to know all the dirt.

The Nephilim live after the flood as the enemy, that is, as some of the indigenous peoples. The flood gets rid of the mutated race of giants—but not quite—they reappear, for example, in Numbers 13 and 1 Samuel 17 (Goliath). Walter Stephens defines "giants" as those beings that "embody the forces that resist expansion, conquest, cultivation, and domestication. Because they oppose the origin of a culture, they are envisioned as archaic, even autochthonic; they are an explanation of origins made by cultures that see themselves as invaders or latecomers" (1989: 73–3, in Gay 1995: 357). Giants bring destruction and make victory over them even greater, especially when the political stability is tenuous. These foreign, pagan giants deserved to be destroyed due to their unbridled sexuality and immorality, and besides, they were probably uncircumcised, too. Von Rad admits, "Possibly in the ancient myth even the widespread motif of a god's envy played a role" (1972: 115).

A myth, a fantastic story, has been made into a horrific narrative of another fall of humanity. Scholars overwhelmingly read this story as horror literature. Roger Schlobin relates the sense of horror:

Deep horror's closed, nihilistic cosmos is filled with seemingly countless mutations:

evolution	de-evolution
hope	futility
promises	lies
salvation	annihilation
eros	lust
overtures	plots
sensuality	the erotic and pornographic
sexuality	aggressiveness
intimacy	intrusion
seduction	rape
relationships	traps
nurturing	oppression
opportunity	despair
expectation	despite
freedom	bondage

(1988: 34)

When evil comes from the divine realm in the Bible, it is excessive and out of human control. Only God can restore order and hope. There is no hope for a return to Eden; the possibility of immortality is lost forever.

Divine intervention: the colonized body of the daughters of men

Is this tale of divine marriage a tale of enchantment and romance? Or is it a tale of alien monsters and the subjugation of women? Certainly the story provides a new twist on the divine–human encounter. The details of the lives of the characters are missing, unlike (to give one example) the many retellings of *Beauty and the Beast*. Genesis 6 shares several features with this and other fairy tales: "Beauty is the highest value for women;" "Males should be aggressive and shrewd;" "Magic and miracles are the means by which social problems are resolved" (Zipes 1987: 6). Marina Warner says of *Beauty and the Beast* that the Beast represents, "a sign of authentic, fully realized sexuality, which women must learn to accept if they are to become normal adult heterosexuals" (1994: 312). The divine beings might not be monsters, but they are aliens, even if they took on human form.

Women are displaced (Spivak 1983) in multiple ways in Genesis 6. Why the focus on the *beauty* of the women? Are they to be seen as the promiscuous counterparts of the virgin goddess Istahar (or Ishtar/Aphrodite/Venus) who escapes from the sons of God to seek refuge with God, who makes her into the constellation Virgo (Graves and Patai 1963: 101)? Does the focus on their beauty imply their active seduction of the sons of God? Or is this focus part of the displacement of the daughters? Are these women *femme fatales*? According to most commentators who read Genesis 6 through its apocryphal retellings (especially 1 Enoch), these women are responsible for God enacting evil on humankind. The reader gazes on the women as the divine beings do. Their beauty enchants and is mysterious.

The daughters are displaced in the text (as generic objects of beauty and reproductive usefulness), but even more so in the patriarchal interpretations. In the text their wombs are fertile. These women are able to give birth to *giants*, making them gynecologically superior(!). But their wombs could be the breeding place of men of devastation (see Creed 1993: 53ff). In "the social text of motherhood" (Spivak 1983: 190) these daughters have no place of honor; they have no names and no voices and no mothers. The absent mother is a frequent theme in fairy tales. In the cosmic disaster that follows, the women of Noah's family have no names. The flood becomes the ultimate displacement of the women.

Heaven is excessive; the heavenly realm extends to and through human women. The border between heaven and earth is transgressed. We are not told if the women had a choice in their marriage to the angels. Are the angels God's colonizers? Is this a story about alien abduction/*in*vasion? Are the sons of Elohim rulers in the sense that they are colonizers of the earth through human women? Ann Stoler relates that *desire* is a strong aspect of the colonial order. She states:

> But once we turn to question the distributions of desires, to "discover who does the speaking" in the geopolitical mapping of desiring and desired objects, "our part of the world" becomes more than an innocuous convention, but a porous and problematic boundary to sustain. For that boundary itself, as we know, took as much discursive and

political energy to produce as that which bound sex to
power, and the "truth" of identity to sex.

(1995: 167)

In the Bible humans cannot sustain the boundary between heaven
and earth, and power and desire are linked. In this story of divine
colonization God is also not able to sustain the boundary; the divine
beings cross over—God crosses over. Some questions remain: is this
divine marriage all right with God? Does God think human women
are evil? Does God have morals? Is heaven a moral realm?

Are these divine beings an extension of God's phallus, like the
angel Gabriel in the annunciation of Mary scene? Is this possibly
unsanctioned birth (or demonic birth in apocryphal works), for
Christian readers at least, opposed to the holy birth of Jesus? The
Nephilim may be partially divine, and thus share a dual identity, like
Jesus. I see a connection with the annunciation story in Luke. A male
deity impregnates Mary. This activity is only acceptable in the case of
the annunciation of a virgin for the birth of the messiah. In Genesis 6
an aberration has occurred; no acceptable giant (such as Samson) is
born, and certainly no messiah appears. In the contemporary angel
craze in the USA (evidenced, for example, in television shows such as,
Highway to Heaven and *Touched by an Angel*) angels never have sex with
humans, yet the actors who play the angels are highly sexualized.
What does the encounter with angels mean for women in the Bible?
Does the male God occasionally desire human women? Is this what
the Bible is saying?

In another direction, does the reader repress desire for the Other—
the divine, supernatural being? The women are not burned up in
angelic fire, for the celestial beings apparently take human form.
They reproduce giant *sons* in a culture that valued male progeny above
all. The Nephilim share God's power, at least for 120 (three generations of forty) years. Is there reflected in this story an anxiety in the
extreme over intermarriages with foreigners? Instead of the usual
women foreigners (e.g. Ruth), the men are foreign (as in Esther, but
she is in the Diaspora and it is for a good cause). In Genesis 6 the
foreign men are really, *really* foreign.

Is Genesis 6: 1–4 a transformed matriarchal tale? In other words,
did later patriarchal cultures change an early woman-centered myth?
Zipes points out that in fantasy literature "the impulse and critique of
the 'magic' are rooted in a historically explicable desire to overcome
oppression and change society" (1988: 8). Perhaps there is a trace of
the desire for magic in order to change the social order. Feminist

biblical scholars point to the dominant patriarchal tradition and retrace the narrative through its phallocentric hermeneutical history. Ilona Rashkow believes that "the narrative begins a long tradition of attributing the origin of evil: here, as elsewhere, the problem revolves around women positionally coded as 'daughters'" (1993: 80). Mieke Bal makes a similar statement: "Should we conclude, then, that the ideology of the Hebrew Bible has it that women should be avoided, that love kills the man who is its victim? Modern readings of the stories seem to believe it does" (1987: 131). Is this relationship then "lethal"? In Genesis 6 there is no mention of love; even so the heavenly males are defiled (1 Enoch) and (almost) all of the products of the unions are destroyed. In the context of the whole of Genesis eroticism brings death (Bataille 1986).

Conclusion: leaving heaven

A love story

If Genesis 6: 1–4 stood alone, it would have the possibility of a happy ending. Since happy endings are a feature of fairy tales, I want to explore this opening in the text. Zipes relates that fairy tales have a liberatory function, and I wonder if one reading of Genesis 6: 1–4 could be as liberatory. Zipes explains: "This does not mean that the liberating fairy tale must have a moral, doctrinaire resolution, but that, to be liberating, it must reflect *a process of struggle* against all types of suppression and authoritarianism and posit various possibilities for the concrete realization of utopia" (1988: 178). Fairy tales cross the boundaries of all norms of race, class, gender and sexuality, and this Genesis story slips through all attempts to determine its meaning.

Why are interpreters fearful of the fantastic and so wary of this story? The dominant exegetical mode is to bring the narrative under control: to isolate it and bind it in traditional historical critical method, ancient Near Eastern comparisons and early dates so as to remove it from more "authentic" material. Myth is necessary and important in cultures, and many interpretations miss the *story* altogether.

Roland Barthes speaks about this necessity for myth:

> It would seem that we are condemned for some time yet to speak *excessively* about reality. This is probably because ideologism and its opposite are types of behaviour which are still

magical, terrorized, blinded and fascinated by a split in the
social world.

(1972: 159)

This myth of Genesis 6 continues to speak and provide support to
patriarchal systems of oppression. This story is told and retold from
many starting points in other texts (1 Enoch, Josephus, Augustine,
etc.). There is a sense that because this story is embarrassing and odd
(to name a few slurs that have been made on it) that it is allowable to
play around with it. Most of the play has been within the confines of
the traditional historical critical method and/or the perpetuation of
misogynistic readings. But there are many (indeterminate) paths of
this short "sudden fiction," and I want to play with the concepts of
the fantastic, horror, fairy tales and feminist midrash. Here are a few
experimental versions of Genesis 6: 1–4:

Poetry version

displaced daughters
give birth to giants
no names no voices
no mothers
heaven is excessive
God crosses over

(Gene Doty)

Disney version

Once upon a time there was a rich king with ten beautiful daughters.
The daughters were so beautiful that they were renowned in all the
land. Now there was an evil sorcerer who had put a curse on the king's
beloved wife, and she died after giving birth to the last child. The
beautiful daughters were then taken by the evil sorcerer who kept
them locked up in his hidden castle, to be stuck in a tormentuous
marriage to his ten demonic sons, whose plan was to force them to
give birth to demon progeny. The daughters were not only beautiful,
but intelligent and strong-willed, and they plotted to escape. On
their wedding night they spiked the wedding wine (with the help of
the local witch); the demon husbands fell fast asleep and the women
stole their husbands' wings and flew away.

Stephen King version

And it came to pass in a small coastal village that a strange man moved to town with his sons and set up a mysterious shipping business on the harbor. Before too long women in the town began gathering at the business, but in twos and threes, so as not to draw suspicion. Eventually all the women in the town disappeared on the boats, but then giant demon children appeared, the ones who brought devastation on the town.

Brothers Grimm version

Once upon a time there lived a poor farmer who was barely able to grow enough crops to feed his ten daughters. These daughters were the most beautiful women of this country. After his wife died giving birth to the tenth daughter, the farmer was forced to sell his small plot of land to the evil king who ruled over all this country. Now the king was fond of beautiful women and he collected them as diligently as he collected land. Since the farmer needed all his daughters to work the farm, he was not able to hide them. One summer's day the king passed by the tiny farm in his grand carriage of gold, and he saw the ten beautiful daughters and lusted greatly after them. He took them into his castle, and these daughters gave birth to ten sons each, who eventually overthrew their father the evil king. The women and their sons became the renowned farmers of old, giving the land back to the people and overseeing the distribution of wealth justly.

One possible feminist version

And it came to pass that the male deities came to earth and mated with the daughters of men. The daughters of men preferred these supernatural men to their human patriarchs who beat them and blamed them for bringing sin into the world. Besides, the sex was incredible! They gave birth to giant warrior sons who began to take over the world. So the king of the male deities became nervous of their great power and limited their lives to 120 years. These women also secretly gave birth to amazon daughters. These daughters, knowing good and evil, left the earthly conquest to their brothers, but they and their mothers stormed heaven (with a magical ladder from the goddess Ishtar who had lost her position in the downsizing of heaven by Elohim), where they live eternally, wise women of renown.

4

PRESENTING THE POISON
IN THE GOSPEL OF JOHN

Jorunn Jacobsen Buckley

... the elements of the gift, the obligation to receive and the
obligation to make a return.

(Marcel Mauss, *The Gift*)

The core of this study centers around Jesus' poisoning of Judas in
chapter 13 of the gospel of John. To my knowledge, Jesus' feeding
Judas the dipped morsel at the meal of the Last Supper has never been
treated as a poisoning. In order to substantiate this new interpretation, I will draw attention to chosen, recurrent patterns in John's
gospel, patterns of inclusion and exclusion and of violent swings
between salvation and perdition. Jesus' words and actions frequently
exhibit a powerful paradoxality, an intended doubleness different
from the traditionally understood "spiritual vs. material" meanings.
Rather, these twin messages carry an explosive polemical power of
simultaneity, which collapses common dualistic patterns such as
"spiritual vs. real," as if one were free to choose between the two.
Water, bread, light, etc.—all cherished, well-known examples of
John's favored images of Jesus—instead demand unswerving acceptance on both levels.

To pay attention to the gospel's dynamism, its images of acute,
oppositional simultaneity of meanings, requires a mindset attuned to
salvific action revealing its very reverse. John's obsession with
polemics fits into the picture of violence, as does the menacing under-
tone in some of the miracles. In addition to treating these uneasy
issues, I will also deal with a couple of commonly concealed meanings
of important words in the text. The overarching topic, however,
remains God's plan for Jesus, which requires the activity of Satan. In
manipulating Judas, Jesus ensures a collaboration between good and

evil, even a merging of God and Satan, a dynamic that allows sadism to emerge as a central point in the plan of salvation.

It is hardly news to interpret the disciple Judas less as a villain, more as a positive, yet deeply tragic figure. W. Klassen's (1996) book is the latest example. Previously, German scholars in particular have been able to give varied, nuanced portraits of Judas (Klauck 1987; Wrede 1907). Limbeck calls Judas' act a "salvific betrayal"—the very title of the work in which his study appears—and quotes P. Berthold, who states that "without Judas, no cross; without the cross, no fulfillment of the salvation plan" (Limbeck 1976: 85).[1] And Schwarz considers it unconscionable to associate Judas with betrayal (1988: 228).

But none have asked the simple question of what the scene between Jesus and Judas most resembles. Were it not secured within the double fences of the "sacred scripture" and the Last Supper, the incidence as an indisputable poisoning might have sprung immediately to anyone's mind. In the following chapter, I first present the poisoning scene; next, I pay attention to the verb "to trouble" (Greek: *tarassein*), which occurs at key instances in the gospel. Then comes a treatment of food and of opposed kinds of eating—regular and mastication—found in the text; further, a section on the gospel's structural switches in selected images on miracles and polemics; and finally, a return to the poisoning scene, with concluding remarks.

The climax of chapter 13

The meal called the Last Supper occurs, says John, before the feast of Passover. It is significant that John presents no Eucharist; the footwashing instead seems to take its role. That the devil has already put it into Judas' heart to hand Jesus over to the authorities is an event preceding the meal itself, according to Gospel of John 13: 2. I adhere to the translation "to hand over" instead of "betray"[2] for *paradidonai*, in accordance with Klassen's major argument in his rich, recent work on Judas. Even though the expression "put into the heart" can be understood to mean "to plan" (1996: 148), I will keep in mind the word "heart" because of the gospel's interest in anatomy and physiology.

Jesus interrupts the supper to wash the disciples' feet, obviously including those of Judas. I will return to the footwashing later, but one might note at this point that the act carries the warring symbolic significance of both inclusion and exclusion. Cryptically, Jesus says that even the baptized need to have their feet washed. The disciples

ought not to be scandalized by Jesus' inverting the hierarchical structure, his taking a servant's role, for the washing makes the disciples
part of Jesus. It remains separate from baptism, a ritual here evaluated
as strangely incomplete, for not all of the baptized are clean, Jesus
hints.

Without naming him, Jesus has selected Judas (John 13: 18), and
"troubled in spirit" (John 13: 21) prepares to display the chosen one
to the rest of the disciples. John obviously plays with the possibility
that the unnamed bosom friend (John 13: 23, 25), tantalizingly
portrayed in the closest proximity to Jesus, *might* be intended.
However, suspicion is quickly deflected from this disciple, although
Peter thinks that the bosom friend knows Jesus' target, but he does
not and, seemingly innocently, asks Jesus (John 13: 24–5). Tension
mounts as anxiety and suspicions deepen among the disciples. On the
surface, this is classical division tactics from Jesus' side. Avoiding
naming and continuing to be theatrically and threateningly indirect,
Jesus gives the dipped morsel to Judas.

As a result of the food, "after the morsel" (John 13: 27), Satan
enters Judas, which I take as a direct poisoning. Recall that Satan had
already influenced Judas' heart (John 13: 2). Now, Jesus ensures that
Satan also enters Judas on a deeper level, into his guts, his digestive
system. Wrede (1907), too, notes that eating marks a more definitive
step than something simply being put "into the heart" (1907: 136).
A plan harbored in the heart may change, but eating satanic food
implies a suffusion, a spreading of its effects into the whole body. In
order to guarantee that the divine plan will be carried out, Jesus must
perform sorcery on Judas. After eating the morsel, Judas "hurls
himself . . . into the night," says Wrede (1907: 136). But this
comment seems misguided, for the specification "it was night" (John
13: 30) instead emphasizes the night as a striking result of the eating.
This sudden darkness underscores the end of the salvific work,
because in John 9: 4 Jesus has already taught about night and day. *His*
work belongs to the day, not to the night, which descends as Judas
exits. *Judas'* duty, in contrast, is just beginning.

It is instructive to note that the other disciples are completely
ignorant of the import of Jesus' last words to Judas, "What you are
going to do, do quickly" (John 13: 27). They think that Judas is
being instructed to buy food for the feast, or to give an offering to the
poor (John 13: 29). So, John, with characteristic dramatic flair,
protracts the distance between the non-comprehending disciples and
the tight team made up of Jesus and Judas. Wrede recalls the gnostic
Cainites, who interpreted Judas as the only insider, the real "knowl-

edgeable one" among Jesus' disciples (1907: 133). This scholar also sees Jesus as pressuring Judas to betray him, which leaves Judas guilt free, though John does not see matters in this light, says Wrede (1907: 136). But I think John deliberately insists on the tension, inviting an interpretation that accepts the paradox. One must assume that Judas has known all along that Jesus would set in motion a special scenario for him, although perhaps not exactly *how* this would occur.

To trouble

The verb *tarassein*, meaning "to trouble," "to stir up", "to throw into disorder," is used in John when profound change, for better or for worse, is imminent. I take the verb to be parable-indicating, as parables usually display transformations demanding acceptance as both natural and miraculous. I will attend to John 5: 7 first. A multitude of afflicted people throng near the pool Bethsatha ("pool of mercy") at the Sheep Gate, waiting for an angel to trouble the water so that healing may occur. Jesus converses with a lame man, who is unhappy because others prevent him from entering the water at the crucial time of stirring. But Jesus heals him simply by his word, rendering the water unnecessary.

The story is sheer anti-Jewish polemic. Cullmann (1978: 86) rightly observes that Jesus takes the place of the angel who periodically disturbs the water. However, Cullmann fails to note an important point, for it is not merely an issue of replacement but of conflating subject and object. The angel stirs the water, but Jesus stirs nothing, needing no external substance. He himself is, as he says elsewhere in one of John's favorite images, the living water. Thus, the focus is on Jesus, his word and its power to effect drastic change. He has, so to speak, stirred up himself, activated his double capacity as healer and healing matter. This positive healing story deals a nasty blow to Judaism and its traditional understanding of salvific agents.

There is another healing pool in John, the one called Siloam (chapter 9). After Jesus has smeared a blind man's eyes with clay made of Jesus' own spittle, he tells him to wash in Siloam (John 9: 6). At first this might seem like a concession to Judaism, and one may wonder whether the lesson of the Bethsatha pool, in chapter 5, has been forgotten. But the story is not necessarily an attempt at balancing a traditional view of healing with a new one, for the meaning of the pool's name is "sent." "Siloam" conceals what is obvious in, for instance, Syriac, which preserves the form "sent":

Shiluha. Again, Jesus claims himself as the healing substance, not just the healing agent. But John plays on ambiguities, for the healed man, uncomprehending, goes off and by showing himself to the priest (as Jesus has demanded) obediently follows Jewish custom. The man seems not to know that Jesus is the real water. Without Jesus' spittle—another liquid, a kind of internal water—the miracle obviously could not work.

"Let not your hearts be troubled (*tarassestho*)" (John 14: 1), says Jesus to the disciples immediately after severely upsetting Peter by predicting Peter's denial of him. This, not Judas' act, will be the true betrayal. An almost unbearable tension emerges here, as Jesus tells Peter that even if Peter may, at some future point, lay down his life for Jesus—as he has grandly promised—the most glaring act will be his denying that he knew Jesus at all. Literally in the next breath come Jesus' words "let not your hearts be troubled," which in the context appear almost vicious. To command the disciples to believe in God and not to be anxious seems, in this setting, absurd and far from consoling.

Three times Jesus, facing great difficulties, is described as being in emotional turmoil. Troubled in his spirit and in his soul, Jesus gives expression to an embedded anthropological model that unfortunately remains non-explicit in the gospel. The weeping Mary, who is attended by other mourning Jews, complains that if Jesus had been present, her brother Lazarus would not have died. Now, Jesus is "deeply moved in spirit and troubled" (John 11: 38), conveyed by the Greek verbal expressions *enebrimesato* ("groaned") and *etaraxen eauton* ("troubled himself"). The verses 31–8 contain an extraordinary piling up of verbs expressing psychological disturbance. "Groaning in himself" (to follow the Greek), in John 11: 38, Jesus approaches Lazarus' tomb. This inner, violent stirring seems to be a prerequisite for salvation, in this case the most impressive of all: a raising from the dead. Jesus' internal turbulence at this scene recalls the troubled water in chapter 5.

In John's sequence of events, trouble intensifies as Passover nears. Some Greeks wishing to worship at the feast in Jerusalem and to see Jesus, approach his disciple Philip (John 12: 21). In full public view, Jesus makes strong allusions to his own end and admits that "now is my soul troubled" (*tetaraktai*), in John 12: 27. After uttering the possibility that he might beg God to be saved "from his hour" (John 13: 27), Jesus instead asks the Father to glorify his name. And the reassuring voice comes from heaven, "I have glorified it, and will glorify it again." Some hear the words as a thunderclap, others interpret the noise as an angel speaking to Jesus. Evidently, none other than Jesus have heard the words for what they are: a judgment on the world. But this momentous incident meets with an almost total lack of comprehension. The isolated, troubled healer stands worlds apart from the crowd.

In parallel, one may recall the pattern from the poisoning scene, in which the disciples (aside from Judas) did not understand Jesus' words but made their own, irrelevant interpretation of them. It is hardly by chance that John follows the same pattern here in the scene featuring the alien voice from heaven. Increasingly, one notes that Jesus, when emphasized as troubled, is a figure facing immense difficulties in utterly lonely knowledge and determination.

However, in chapter 13, Judas, alone among the disciples, does understand what Jesus does to him. Jesus' speech following the foot washing includes hints to Judas' role and ends with a command to receive those whom Jesus will send. Finished with this speech, Jesus is "troubled in spirit" and immediately testifies that "one of you will hand me over" (John 13: 21). At this, the disciples look at one another, uncertain. But Jesus and Judas know what is happening, and the poisoning will ensure that events take their preappointed course.

Klassen states that Jesus' "deep agitation of spirit" from John 13: 21 results from the insult he suffers at Judas, "a friend who has just eaten with him" (1996: 148). But, this interpretation neglects the sequence, which stresses the agitation as preparatory to the feeding, for Jesus is troubled (*tarasso*) *before* he gives Judas the morsel. Again, the troubling in and of the agent is a prerequisite for momentous change and in full accordance with God's plan.

Whatever the two, Jesus and Judas, ate together before this incident, is of no concern to the gospel writer, for it is the dipped morsel that counts. One also wonders why Klassen, who is interested in defending Judas' acts, at this point uses the word "insult." Klassen's reaction shows how difficult it is to shed negativity towards Judas, despite the scholar's chief argument. Klauck misrepresenting the scene, thinks that Judas has obtained the "eucharistic gift" by deception, "another devilish act of his" (1987: 83).

Two kinds of eating

The Oxford Bible does not differentiate between the commonly used verb, "to eat," *efagein*, and "to masticate," or "to chew to bits," *trōgein*. The former is used in several cases to describe Jewish kinds of eating, while the second is associated with the consuming of Jesus' body.

Those who masticate, eat Jesus and thus become suffused by his essence, while regular feeding results in nothing spectacular. In polemical segments, such eating in the long run becomes outright deadly. So, in John we have what amounts to a technical terminology with regard to eating, terms with drastically different evaluations. Jesus destroyed as food becomes spiritual life for others, whereas the less violently imaged, regular eating merely perpetuates bodily life.

The mass feeding in chapter 6 is a prefiguration of the Last Supper. Even the position of the thousands is reclining—like the disciples do in chapter 13—not sitting, as the Oxford Bible translates. In chapter 6, as in chapter 13, Jesus is prone to perplexing pronouncements, asking Philip how they might possibly buy bread to feed so many (John 6: 5). He is testing him, and the little boy with the five loaves and the two fish then enters the picture. Having given thanks (*eucharistēsas*) for the food, Jesus distributes the now magnified nourishment. Clearly, the food *is* Jesus himself, both bread and fish being symbols of Jesus in John. And the gathered remnants, which Jesus insists must not be scattered, conveniently fit into twelve baskets, the number of the disciples. According to this prefiguration, Jesus' substance continue on in them. The verb *bibróskein*, "to eat up," "gnaw," "consume," is used in v. 13, perhaps a consciously chosen verb to indicate that what the people have eaten was no ordinary meal.

Pursued by the people the next day, Jesus chides them for urging more food miracles. He uses the opportunity to launch an invective against the fathers led by Moses in the wilderness, for they ate heaven-sent manna, but still died (John 6: 49). Contrasting this bread to himself, the true bread from heaven, Jesus again makes a point of fusing agent and object, as he did when he replaced the angel at the pool by the Sheep Gate. Not Moses, but God, gave the Jews the heavenly bread. For Moses was a mere man, one unable to embody the divine substance in himself (John 6: 32–3).

The discourse on food continues, and the Jews of Capernaum grow increasingly agitated as Jesus insists on his position as the bread of life. The verb *trōgein*, "masticate," used exclusively for Jesus, begins to appear in John 6: 54, "he who eats my flesh." Cullmann (1978) is struck by the shocking use of *sarx*, "flesh," instead of the allegedly more palatable *sōma*, "body" (1978: 99), but he does not halt at the verb. When Jesus employs the verb *trōgein*, he is exhorting his hearers to act with urgency; he no longer speaks of a form of eating envisioned in the future. Verse 57 has "he who eats (*trōgōn*) me will live because of me," and in verse 58 the opposition between the two kinds of eating is particularly stark: "not such as the fathers ate (*efagon*) and died, he who eats (*trōgōn*) this bread will live forever."

In chapter 13, too, the verb occurs as Jesus, quoting Psalm 41: 9, speaks of Judas, "He who ate (*trōgōn*) my food has lifted his heel against me" (John 13: 18). And what kind of food will Judas eat? The word "morsel," *psōmion*—like the word *klasmata* used for the leftover fragments of the mass feeding in chapter 6—does not catch the clue in either story. Consulting the Syriac version of John, one notes that "bread," *lahma*, is used on both occasions, no crumbs or morsels.

Not only is Jesus the bread, but the dipped bread presented to Judas is essentially a baptized body. For the verb "to dip" is the same as the verb "to baptize." In my opinion, then, Judas obtains a "baptized Jesus," i.e. a clean body, in order to furnish him, Judas, with the purity apparently denied him in Jesus' cryptic statement, "you are clean, but not every one of you" (John 13: 19). This does not contradict my main notion that the scene is one of poisoning, for in keeping with John's fondness for double messages, both remain valid. Feeding Judas, Jesus simultaneously curses and heals him.

Several years ago, when I first pondered these paradoxes, Professor David Frankfurter, a specialist on early Christianity and other religions in late antiquity Egypt, appeared in a dream of mine in which the two of us discussed these issues (this is no joke). As I insisted that the poisoning act denotes a willed dissociation from Jesus, David Frankfurter just as emphatically held on to the view that Judas still remains within the realm of salvation, still has a part in Jesus. In the dream, I came to agree, holding on to *both* positions, which I continue to do.

Structures and switches

Water is turned into wine in chapter 2, while salvific food becomes poison in chapter 13. The prelude to the poisoning, the footwashing, merits attention because it takes the place of any expected eucharist. John says nothing of other disciples being fed with a dipped piece of bread, but all of them have their feet washed. It is likely that John, ever mindful of parallel set-ups, invites the reader to think back to chapter 12, to Mary, who six days before Passover anoints Jesus' feet and then wipes them with her hair (John 12: 3). Now, preparing to wash his disciples' feet, Jesus loosens the towel wrapped around his waist—a cloth containing his own emanated bodily, salvific power—to dry their wet feet.

In chapter 12, Judas was scandalized at the alleged waste of the expensive oil, while now, in chapter 13, Peter bristles at Jesus reversing the master/slave structure. Neither disciple catches what is happening: the prefiguration for Jesus' burial and the literal membership in Jesus conferred by the footwashing. Jesus differentiates between washing and bathing (i.e. baptism), but he stresses that even the baptized need to have their feet washed (John 13: 10). Why is this necessary?

Baptismal water in all likelihood is understood as a form of cleansing by which the dirt slips off the body from the head down. Foot washing concentrates on the opposite direction, as a type of inoculation and slow suffusion, because salvific water applied at the feet travels upwards (see Brown 1991: 348–9). All, Judas included, now have a part in Jesus, but Judas, because of the planned poisoning, may need the water's healing capacities even more than the other disciples. The water is applied to him as a counterforce to the effects of the satanic food, the dipped bread carrying its double weight. The link between food and water is this: as internal and external waters are stirred, so food agitates the body into life-giving change.

Knowing that, in one sense, Judas is not—indeed, cannot be— clean (John 13: 11) because he will hand Jesus over, Jesus still washes him and at no point reprimands Judas for the role meted out to him. Such a reproach would have been absurd, Judas' act being a necessary sin. Jesus himself drives Judas to it, as Wrede notices (1907: 136).

So, purity emerges as a tricky, delicately negotiable issue in chapter 13. Busy with his basin and towel, Jesus includes Judas, appointed to run Satan's errand. Increasingly interchangeable, God, Jesus, and Satan indeed appear to work together in a scheme requiring destruction and violence in order to achieve salvation. (That God and Satan may be partners is no news; it is familiar to readers of the Book of Job.) According to the logic of magic, the bread must enter, masticated, into Judas' digestive system. Jesus himself, chewed into fragments, will act in Judas. One may recall here Syrian Jacobite regulations for making and then breaking the holy bread along specific lines baked into it. Broken apart, the pieces are then aligned into arrangements in the likeness of a human being. Thus Jesus is re-created from the fragments (Drower 1956: 144–6).

What would be truly Satanic is Judas avoiding his duty. Jesus accuses the Jews of having the devil as their father (John 8: 44), whereas he, Jesus, claims God as his own father. The Jews' will is to do their father's, the devil's, desires (John 8: 44), while Jesus claims that his food—a significant choice of metaphor—is to do the will of the one who sent him (John 4: 34). Judas must straddle the demarcation line between the vilified Judaism and belief in Jesus, because Jesus himself arranges events to this effect.

As a believer, Judas has undoubtedly drunk of the living waters flowing out of Jesus' cavity (John 7: 38)—"heart" is a slanted mistranslation. These waters are directed towards those flowing out of his side after the crucifixion. John interprets these fluids as the Spirit, which, he specifies, will not be distributed before Jesus' glorification (this happens—or is prefigured—in chapter 12, as we have seen). Judas also eats the dipped bread, the baptized Jesus, a meal that for Judas alone becomes a "satanic sacrament" (Wrede 1907: 136). To the other disciples the meal is apparently harmless, although John does not specify individual disciples receiving bread from Jesus' hand at the meal.

Concluding remarks

As Jesus, at the scene of arrest, tells his imprisoners to let the disciples go, his words fulfill the alleged prediction that none among them is lost (John 18: 8–9). Klassen (1996), noting the discrepancy between this statement and John 17: 12, which excludes "the son of perdition," sees this as an example of John's bad editing skills but good dramatic sense (1996: 142). But the apparent contradiction might rather be appreciated as an intended doubleness, for Judas is "lost" in a surface sense, but on another, deeper level, he is the closest to Jesus precisely because he has fully played his destructive role.

Klassen seems to me too divisively dualistic in his assertion that, "it would have been wholly inconsistent with the mission of Jesus for him to drive demons out of other people's lives and free them from bondage to Satan while allowing his own disciple, Judas, to be possessed of Satan" (1996: 143). On the contrary, only by ensuring that Judas is poisoned, at least for a duration sufficient to fulfill his task, can Jesus keep control over God's plan for them both. Elsewhere, Klassen rightly notices that Judas acts "more like an automaton than a free, willing person" (1996: 153). This is so because the dipped morsel has deprived him of his regular sense and secular judgment, which in all likelihood would have halted him in his tracks.

Subject and object merge as Judas receives the baptized Jesus and returns the poisoned blessing by handing Jesus over to the authorities. This is fully in accordance with the divine plan. As the contract between Jesus and Judas is honored, the circle closes. In both movements—the giving and the return of the present—the gift is Jesus himself, a collapsed giver and gift, in keeping with John's predilection for such conflation, especially in healing scenes.

As far as power is concerned, there is no structural discrepancy between sorcery and miracles. Both kinds of feats evoke and manipulate supernatural forces, and power itself is neutral, harnessed for good or for evil. Jesus certainly is capable of doing both, like any wonder worker and/or shaman. His being troubled at the threshold of certain momentous incidences, as we have seen, also fits with the well-known pattern of shamanic depression, which prescribes the worker's own suffering as a required correlate to that of his patients. Literally, the healer/magician must carry the illnesses of his clients. The "suffering servant" language known from Isaiah may well be shamanic.

Had John been interested in mentioning Judas' death—which he is not—he might have portrayed him as perishing from sheer overload of paradoxical symbolism. Unlike others, I am not particularly interested in "what really happened," as in the current scholarly near-obsession with the retrieval of a historical Jesus. But from a mythological standpoint the story of Jesus feeding Judas provides an instructive angle for interpreting recurrent dramatic structures in the gospel. In dual opposition to the present drive for historicity and also to the old Bultmannian de-mythologizing program, I would instead call for renewed energies in the task of re-mythologizing the gospels and other New Testament writings. John's story of Jesus and Judas provides an exceptionally demanding myth resistant to judgmental interpretations based on a facile "either–or" dualism.

Were New Testament scholarship again to place mythology at its center, we might expect wholly new approaches to symbolism and structures, to repeated and inverted parallels. John's Jesus may heal as he destroys, and vice versa, and John's profound appreciation of paradox produces titillating dynamics, rather than static dualism. In my view, John as a paradox-driven myth-maker invites new, thorough imaginings. To abolish the "either–or" in favor of the "both–and" of apparent contradictions may seem to belong to the category of faith alone. But it is a requirement of scholarly investigations into early Christian texts, too, if one is to accept scholars' claims that they take seriously gospel writers such as John.

These days, much energy is spent on reconstructing the so-called historical Jesus, a noble enough exercise, but one that carries with it a peculiar danger of fundamentalism: worship of history at the expense of the mythological imaginations at work in the New Testament writers. In a comparative perspective, with due lessons from anthropology, from literary criticism, and the dual histories of the imagination and of religions, New Testament scholarship still has much to accomplish. Interdisciplinary models may offer useful ways to interpret sorcery and salvation, and, as in the present case, the body and its life as "natural symbols"—to re-iterate Mary Douglas' (1970) term. However, in calling for investigations of individual imaginations—ranging from the coolly philosophical to the hot-headed apocalyptic—I would also urge caution, when invoking anthropology, against viewing social models and structures as sufficient in interdisciplinary experiments for New Testament studies.

Notes

1 Here and in what follows, translations of quotes from the German are my own.
2 My references to and quotations from John's gospel come from *The New Oxford Annotated Bible*.

5

JESUS' VIOLENCE

George Aichele

> In a guessing game to which the answer is chess, which word
> is the only one prohibited?
> The word is *chess*.
> The rules of the game forbid the use of the word itself. To
> eliminate a word completely, to refer to it by means of inept
> phrases and obvious paraphrases, is perhaps the best way of
> drawing attention to it.
>
> (Borges 1962: 99–100)

Jorge Luis Borges' story, "The Garden of Forking Paths" (in Borges
1962) suggests that certain stories function as "guessing games" for
words that never actually appear in the text. The biblical gospel of
Mark is such a story, and one answer to the mysterious guessing game
that is the gospel of Mark is the word *violence*. In the story of Mark, the
character named Jesus is the man of violence. Furthermore, precisely
because Jesus' violence in Mark is mysterious or fantastical—because
Jesus is fantastical in the gospel of Mark—his violence is especially
disturbing to any attempt to guess the meaning of Mark.

A peculiar saying

> From the days of John the Baptist until now the Kingdom of
> Heaven has been forced (*biazetai*) and the violent (*biastai*)
> have seized it. For all the prophets, and the law, prophesied
> until John; and if you wish to accept it, he himself is Elijah,
> who was to come.
>
> (Matthew 11: 12–14)[1]

The words that the gospel of Matthew uses in this saying of Jesus are
rare in the New Testament. The Greek noun *biastês*, "violent ones,"
appears only in this text in Matthew. The Greek verb *biazô*, "to use

force, act with violence," appears only here and in one other text that many consider to be another version of the same saying. This other text appears in the gospel of Luke:[2]

> Until John, it was the law and the prophets; but from then on the good news of the Kingdom of God is announced, and everyone tries to force his way (*biazetai*) into it.
>
> (Luke 16: 16)

The related Greek words *bia* ("violence") and *biaios* ("violent") appear only a few times in the New Testament, all of them in the Acts of the Apostles (2: 2, 5: 26, 21: 35 and 27: 41). Acts 2: 2 describes the Spirit of God arriving on Pentecost like a violent wind, but otherwise these passages do not seem particularly relevant to the issue of violence against the kingdom of God. Nowhere else in the New Testament do any of these words appear.

The two sayings in Matthew 11: 12–14 and Luke 16: 16 are generally regarded as deriving from a single saying in the early Jesus traditions, a saying which appears in the "synoptic sayings source," or "Q." Q (from the German word *Quelle*, "source") is the name given by scholars to the hypothesized common material used by the authors of the gospels of Matthew and Luke in addition to material from the gospel of Mark. In both versions of the saying, the statement about violence against the kingdom of God is presented as a saying of Jesus. However, the two versions of the saying appear in quite different contexts in these gospels. Matthew 11: 12 is part of a longer statement to the crowds about John the Baptist. Luke 16: 16 is part of a debate with Pharisees about the law. Matthew 11: 12 asserts that "the violent" have *already* succeeded in entering the kingdom. In contrast, the Lukan context implies that the violence against the kingdom will not succeed: "But it is easier for heaven and earth to pass away than for one letter end of the law to fail" (Luke 16: 17). Although Matthew has another saying (Matthew 5: 18) that is similar to Luke 16: 17, it too is in a remarkably different context.

In neither of these cases is it clear how the statement about violence and the kingdom of God relates to its larger narrative context. Nor does the context of the saying in Q, as that text has been reconstructed by John Kloppenborg (1988), help to clarify the saying. If Q follows the Lukan sequence of sayings, as many scholars (including Kloppenborg) think, then the tentativeness of Luke's version—people are trying to force their way into the kingdom, but the law is unchanging—is supported. However, in contrast to the more tightly organized narrative structures of Matthew and Luke, the relatively loose organization of Q as a list of sayings provides less context for any single saying. Because the saying in Q lacks the clarifying frame of a narrative context, this makes it especially difficult to determine its meaning.

Nevertheless, even within the metatextual context provided by either Matthew or Luke, the saying about violence against the kingdom resists explanation.[3] What is the connection between violence against the kingdom of God and "the law and the prophets"? Jesus appears to claim that the scriptures ("the law and the prophets") have ceased to be authoritative (to "prophesy") since the appearance of John the Baptist. The version of the saying in Matthew identifies John as Elijah, but in a rather odd way, for the phrase, "if you wish to accept it," suggests that John's status as messianic forerunner depends on the will of the audience, which could be either the crowd to which Jesus speaks or the readers of the gospel.

In these sayings John the Baptist appears as an interruption of the authority of the sacred writings, and this continuing interruption has opened the way to violence against the kingdom of God. It would be tempting to regard the saying as referring to the violence done against John the Baptist himself (e.g. Mark 6: 17–28); however, this would require considerable rewriting of either version of the saying. The present is perceived as a time of violence and at least the threat of chaos—a time in which even unjust stewards (Luke 16: 1–9) can enter the kingdom. Nevertheless, Luke 16: 17 denies that "the letter of the law" (the physical shape of the written letters of Torah) will ever be nullified.

The proclamation of the good news of the kingdom (*hê basileia tou theou euaggelizetai*) that has occurred "from the days of John the Baptist until now" is associated with, or at least concurrent with, violence against the kingdom. This announcement of the gospel probably at least includes, and may be restricted to, Jesus' own teachings. In Mark 1: 14–15, Jesus preaches "the gospel of God" (*to euaggelion tou theou*): "the Kingdom of God (*hê basileia tou theou*) is near." If the proclamation of "the good news of the Kingdom of God" is an oral one—Jesus' words are presented as oral ones in the gospels—does this proclamation stand over against the written scriptures, as the character Jesus stands over against the Pharisees in Luke 16: 14ff.? It is not clear in these sayings what Jesus' opinion of the violence against the kingdom is, but he does seem to be associating himself with it. Does Jesus (perhaps along with John the Baptist) stand over and against those ("everyone," Luke 16: 16; "this generation," Matthew 11: 16) who violently assault the kingdom of God? Or is Jesus himself *among* those who seek violently to seize the kingdom?

Each of the synoptic gospels portrays Jesus as a violent man, one who contests violently with others (Pharisees and scribes, his own followers, the crowds, and perhaps even the Romans). Jesus fights with these others over his own role and identity, over the meaning of the scriptures, and also over the kingdom of God. None of the gospels presents Jesus as a violent man both more explicitly and yet more ambiguously and fantastically than does the gospel of Mark. However, Mark never uses the word "violence" (the Greek word *bia* or related terms), and Mark contains no version of the saying from Q about violence against the kingdom of God. Jesus' violence is never described as such in Mark because his violence is an answer to the guessing game that is the gospel of Mark itself.[4] Nevertheless, violence is a significant part of the *unsaid* that provides the ambiguity and indeterminacy that run throughout Mark's narrative, where violence in relation to the kingdom appears in both the words and the deeds of Jesus.

Violent words

> No one can go into the house of the strong man and seize his goods, unless first he binds the strong man; then he can plunder his house.
>
> (Mark 3: 27)

In this saying of Jesus, the violent struggle between the thief and the strong man is apparent, but the relation of this struggle to the kingdom of God is not clear. The house of the strong man is explicitly identified with a kingdom ("divided against itself") by way of Mark 3: 24–5, where "house" is paralleled with "kingdom." Neither the strong man nor the thief is explicitly identified, but in the larger narrative context of Mark's chapter 3 it appears that the strong man is Satan and the thief is Jesus.[5] This house or kingdom appears to be Satan's, not God's. Yet it is the thief who initiates the violence (who "goes into the house") against the strong man. If Jesus is the thief then he is the aggressor against the kingdom, and the implicit identification of Jesus as a thief also identifies him as one who breaks the law ("until John, it was the law and the prophets").

Earlier in Mark, at Jesus' first encounter with an "unclean spirit," the demon says to him, "What is there between us and you, Jesus of

Nazareth? Did you come to destroy us? I know you, who you are, God's holy one" (Mark 1: 24). The demon's question, "Did you come to destroy us?" suggests an apocalyptic confrontation (Nineham 1963: 79), and Jesus responds by "rebuking" (*epetimêsen*) the demon. As it is used in the gospel of Mark, the Greek verb *epitimaô*, "to rebuke," suggests open conflict: "And convulsing him and crying out in a great voice," the demon comes out of the man, and the people are amazed (Mark 1: 26–7). Jesus "binds" the demon with his words, and violence results.

Another saying associating violence and the kingdom, although often overlooked in this connection, is the parable of the seed growing secretly:

> The Kingdom of God is as when a man sows his seed in the ground, and sleeps and wakes night and day, and the seed grows and increases without his knowing it; for of itself the earth bears fruit, first the blade, then the ear, then the full grain in the ear. But when the grain gives its yield, he puts forth the sickle, for the time of harvesting is come.
>
> (Mark 4: 26–9)

This parable is not so overtly violent as the strong man saying is. However, like the seed's growth, the parable itself is mysterious, and multiple possibilities lurk just beneath its bucolic surface. These words are not to be taken at face value; they appear to be codes for something that cannot be said. As with the thief who binds the strong man, neither the man who sows nor the nature of the grain in this saying are identified: how the story refers to Jesus, or to the kingdom of God, is not clear.

Although the harvest image, like many agricultural images in the Bible and other literature, may be a pleasing one to many readers, it implies a necessary violence, the violence of the reaper against the grain. The sowing image also may imply violence, namely, the act of plowing the earth. Since this saying is explicitly a parable of the kingdom, the violent reaping is open to an apocalyptic reading ("the time of harvesting is come"; compare LXX Joel 4: 13). Intertextual resonance with harvest sayings in other gospels, such as the parable of the wheat and the weeds in Matthew 13: 24–30, or the saying of John the Baptist about separating the wheat and the chaff in Matthew 3: 12 and Luke 3: 17, also suggests an apocalyptic reading of Mark 4: 26–9.

However, an apocalyptic interpretation is only one possible

reading of the parable of the seed growing secretly. The saying's intratextual context in chapter 4 of Mark is a series of parables featuring
agricultural or household themes. This series suggests other possible
readings. For example, in Jesus' interpretation of the sower parable,
which occurs a few verses earlier in the same chapter (Mark 4: 14–20),
the seed described in that parable is allegorized as "the word." This
suggests the possibility that Jesus sows the seed by proclaiming the
gospel of the kingdom of God (see again 1: 14–15). In addition,
Richmond Lattimore's (1979) translation of the parable of the seed
growing secretly suggests sexual overtones: the man "sows his seed"
upon the feminine earth (*epi tês gês*), and the grain "gives its yield."
The farmer who "sleeps and wakes" (*egeirêtai*, "rises") may suggest yet
another allegorical reading: one who dies and is resurrected.

These allegorical possibilities suggest a sort of Dionysian reading
that counters the apocalyptic reading mentioned above: the growth of
the word (or kingdom) is mysterious but quite natural—like a child
in the womb. Is the focus of this parable on those who hear the word
now, as these allegories suggest, or is it on the future judgment, as the
apocalyptic reading claims? Each reading "harvests" the "grain" of
the parable, reaping its mystery. Nor does this exhaust all of the
possibilities: still other readings are conceivable.[6] Any reading of a
text such as this parable requires that the reader establishes intra or
intertextual connections, such as the larger Mark 4 context or the
other harvest sayings, to which the immediate text does not explicitly
refer, in order to clarify the parable's meaning.

This unresolvable tension between competing readings is a characteristic of the fantastic, according to Tzvetan Todorov. The reader of
the fantastic narrative, Todorov says, "will reject allegorical as well as
'poetic' interpretations" (1973: 33). In this statement, "poetic" comes
close to Roman Jakobson's notion of the poetic function of language
(1987: 66–9).

> (P)oetic images are not descriptive. . . . they are to be read
> quite literally, on the level of the verbal chain they consti-
> tute, not even on that of their reference. The poetic image is a
> combination of words, not of things, and it is pointless, even
> harmful, to translate this combination into sensory terms.
> (Todorov 1973: 60)

Poetic language is less concerned with extralinguistic meaning or
reference than it is with the pure play of language with itself.
Apocalyptic language draws heavily on the poetic function, and thus

an apocalyptic interpretation of a saying such as this one leans in the direction of the "poetic."

Todorov claims that the fantastic narrative is fictional, as opposed to poetic, and literal, as opposed to allegorical. In other words, the fantastic story is both meaningful and non-symbolic; it appears to refer to reality. However, "[t]he fantastic is that hesitation experienced by a person who knows only the laws of nature, confronting an apparently supernatural event" (Todorov 1973: 25). Todorov defines the fantastic narrative as one which causes the implied reader to hesitate between two alternative genres: the "uncanny" and the "marvelous." The genre-determined identity of the story itself, the nature of the narrative world that it represents, and of the characters in it, is uncertain and indeterminate. Its reference to reality is thus incomplete. The allegorical reading of Mark 4: 26–9 suggests an uncanny world: a world in which the kingdom of God is present in the mysterious growing of seeds. The apocalyptic reading of the parable of the seed growing secretly reveals a marvelous world: a world in which the kingdom will come on the edge of a harvest sickle. The reader hesitates between these two possibilities.

The violence of apocalyptic cataclysm is only hinted at in the parable of the seed growing secretly. This violence appears far more explicitly in chapter 13 of Mark, the "apocalyptic discourse" of Jesus. In Mark 13: 8, in a saying reminiscent of the "kingdom divided against itself" (3: 24), Jesus says, "For nation shall rise up against nation and kingdom against kingdom." This saying is followed by a vivid list of horrible sufferings,[7] including both natural disasters and human persecutions. It describes perhaps the violence of the emergence of the kingdom of God. Jesus' own role in this violence is once again not clear, but he does say that "many will come in my name, saying: I am he. And they will lead many astray" (Mark 13: 6) and "false Christs and false prophets will rise up, and they will present signs and portents to mislead the chosen, if that may be done" (Mark 13: 22).

In this context Jesus also says that "they will see the son of man coming in the clouds with great power and glory; and then he will send out his angels and gather his chosen together from the four winds, from the end of the earth to the end of the sky" (Mark 13: 26–7). This statement is one of many "son of man" sayings that Jesus utters at various points in the gospel of Mark. However, the significance of these sayings is also unclear, for several reasons. In these sayings there appear two sorts of images of violence in relation to the kingdom. One sort of image depicts explicit violence against the son of man himself. This appears in statements such as "the son of man must suffer much and be rejected by the elders and the high priests and the scribes, and be killed, and rise up after three days" (Mark 8: 31). The other sort of image suggests that violence is associated with the apocalyptic coming of the son of man in power, as in 13: 26–7 noted above, or "He who is ashamed of me and my words in this adulterous and sinful generation, of him will the son of man be ashamed when he comes in the glory of his father with the holy angels. . . . Truly I tell you that there are some of those who stand here who will not taste of death until they see the Kingdom of God arrived in power" (Mark 8: 38–9).

One son of man suffers and dies, and the other son of man comes in power with the kingdom of God. In Todorov's (1973) terms, the suffering son of man is uncanny, and the son of man coming with power is marvelous. Can both of these sons of man be one person? The reader hesitates again: are there two different sons of man (one who suffers and another one who comes in power) or is there just one who somehow both suffers and comes in power? Is the son of man an uncanny human being (as in Mark 3: 28) or a marvelous divine one (as in 2: 28)? The uncertainty that results from the two sorts of son-of-man sayings is fantastic, for the reader of the gospel of Mark is given no firm basis for a decision.

It is also unclear whether Jesus himself is the son of man.[8] For example, what is the relation between "me and my words" and "the son of man" in Mark 8: 38? Jesus never says that he is the son of man in the gospel of Mark. Nevertheless, in Mark Jesus himself appears to fulfill the first sort of son-of-man sayings, the sayings about a human, suffering son of man. On the other hand, the son of man who comes in power is always utopian, nowhere to be found in Mark[9] except in Jesus' promises. At the end of the apocalyptic discourse Jesus refuses to say when the catastrophe will occur, but he does say that "this generation will not pass by before all these things are done" (Mark 13: 30; see also 9: 1). It is coming soon. Because the reference of "the son of man" is ambiguous, the connection between the son of man and the kingdom of God in these sayings is also not clear: is it the suffering son's violent death or is it the apocalyptic son's violent arrival in power that brings the kingdom? In either case, the fantastic son of man is aligned with the kingdom of God and suffers or causes violence on its behalf.

Perhaps the most explicit association of violence and the kingdom of God in the words of Jesus in the gospel of Mark appears in the vineyard parable:

A man planted a vineyard and ran a fence about it and dug a pit for the wine press and built a tower, and let it out to farmers and left the country. And when the time came, he sent a slave to the farmers to receive from the farmers some of the fruits of the vineyard. And they took him and lashed him and sent him away empty-handed. And again he sent them another slave; and they broke the head of that one and outraged him. And he sent another; and that one they killed; and many others, lashing some, killing some. He had one more, a beloved son; he was the last he sent them, saying: "They will respect my son." But they, the farmers, said among themselves: "This is the heir. Come, let us kill him and the inheritance will be ours." And they took him and killed him, and threw him out of the vineyard. What will the lord of the vineyard do? He will come and destroy the farmers, and give the vineyard to others.

(Mark 12: 1–9)

The intertextual network provided by the Hebrew scriptures, and especially Isaiah 5, suggests a reading of the vineyard images as an allegory for the kingdoms of Israel and Judah, and likewise a reading of the vineyard owner as God. Read in this way, the parable of the vineyard identifies the proper representative of God. This at any rate is how Jesus' audience in the gospel of Mark understands the parable, for the "high priests and the scribes and the elders" to whom he tells the story "knew that the parable he told was directed against them" (Mark 12: 12).

On this reading the vineyard owner is God, the vineyard is the kingdom of God, and the son is God's "heir"—that is, the son of God, the king of Israel (see Psalm 2: 6–7, Isaiah 9: 6). In other words, as the lawful ruler, the owner's son is the "anointed one"—the messiah or Christ. According to this reading of the vineyard parable, the violent death of the son results in effect from the unjust claim of the vineyard's tenants to be its rightful owners, and that death will be avenged in turn by the vineyard's true owner. Jesus' words refer to a violent conflict between two competing claims to ownership of the vineyard or kingdom. Unlike the parable of the seed growing secretly, in this case the allegorical reading itself points towards apocalyptic judgment.

Once again, other readings of the parable are possible. D.E. Nineham (following C.H. Dodd [1978] and J. Jeremias [1958]) argues that to Jesus' contemporaries a socio-political reading of the story would have been likely. This reading would feature a foreign, perhaps Gentile landlord and disgruntled Judean peasants (1963: 309–10), closer to the realities of first-century Palestine. However, this political reading may not be all that far from the allegorical reading described above. Nevertheless, the nature of the kingdom of God is also uncertain in the gospel of Mark. For both readings of the parable the vineyard is a this-worldly place, Judea. Is the kingdom of God the political and geographical entity known as Judea, or is it not? In other words, is the kingdom a this-worldly, material kingdom, to be gained by political or military violence, or is it an other-worldly, spiritual kingdom, to be gained by obedient piety or faith in divine power? Todorov's (1973) hesitation between the uncanny and the marvelous also appears in this choice between political and spiritual readings of the parable. Theoretically, this alternative need not be exclusive; however, the reading of the vineyard parable requires a decision from the reader.

Furthermore, the tension between spiritual and political readings of the vineyard parable does not end here. The reader's decision made in regard to the kingdom also impacts upon his/her understanding of Jesus' identity. Two chapters later in Mark the high priest asks Jesus point-blank, "Are you the Christ, the son of the Blessed One?" (Mark 14: 61). Here the conflict between claimants to ownership of the vineyard reaches its climax. Jesus' answer to the priest's question again invokes the marvelous son of man who comes with power: "I am he, and you will see the son of man sitting on the right of the power and coming with the clouds of the sky" (Mark 14: 62). This answer leads to Jesus' conviction on a charge of blasphemy and then to his suffering and death that follow. In other words, Jesus' words to the priest lead to the "fulfillment" of his own *suffering* son-of-man sayings. In Mark's story, Jesus' implicit threat of divine violence, in both the vineyard parable and again in his apocalyptic response to the high priest, leads to the priests' politically violent response to Jesus' threat. The conflict centers around the question of who owns or controls the kingdom—that is, who is the Christ, the king of Israel. The uncertainty regarding the kingdom of God and the uncertainty regarding Jesus' identity are violently intertwined.

Violent deeds

(The Gerasene demoniac) had often been bound with chains and fetters, and the chains had been torn apart by him and the fetters pounded to pieces, and no one was strong enough to subdue him. Day long and night long he was among the tombs and the hills, crying aloud and beating himself with stones.

(Mark 5: 4–5)

The gospel of Mark presents hints and occasionally explicit descriptions indicating that Jesus' actions were sometimes violent, especially in relation to the kingdom of God. The violence of the character's actions serves also to emphasize the violence of his words. Jesus' violence is suggested but not explicit in his healing miracles. For example, at Jairus's house, Jesus "drives out" of the house (*ekbalôn*, as though they were demons) the mourners who laugh at him when he denies that Jairus's daughter is dead (Mark 5: 40). The violence with which the demons exit those whom they had formerly possessed when Jesus' commands them to do so (e.g. 1: 26, 9: 20, 26) suggests that Jesus may also be acting violently.

In Mark 5: 1–20 Jesus overpowers the extremely violent demons possessing the Gerasene man and sends them into a nearby herd of pigs, who then stampede into the adjacent lake and drown. This miracle is particularly loaded with socio-political overtones: the pigs (considered unclean by Jews), the demons named after a Roman military unit ("Legion"), and the Jew who heals a Gentile by sending the Legion to the swine. Many of the miracle stories in the gospels seem to have allegorical possibilities—for example, the juxtaposition of the disciples' "blindness" to Jesus' identity in Mark 8 with the story of the healing of a blind man in 8: 22–5. Could the story of the marvelous healing of the Gerasene demoniac be the radically transformed account of a rather different event—perhaps even an uncanny attack on some Roman soldiers?

The response of the Gerasene man's neighbors, when they see the man "sitting clothed and in his right mind" (Mark 5: 15), is to beg Jesus to leave their neighborhood. Do the Gerasenes fear military reprisal? If Jesus' kingdom is "not of this world," as John 18: 36 says and as many people understand all of the gospels to say, then why should the Gerasenes desire him to go? As was noted above, Todorov's hesitation between the uncanny and the marvelous can also be understood in these texts as a hesitation between the political and the spiritual. It is once again a question of Jesus' identity: is he a holy man only interested in spiritual matters, or is he a political activist of some sort? There is a strong connection between this issue and the question concerning whether Jesus is the Christ—that is, Jesus' relation to the kingdom of God.

Jesus' violence is still more strongly implied by the story of his arrest and execution. He is arrested at night by an armed crowd "as if I were a highwayman" (Mark 14: 48).[10] Some commentators suggest that Jesus' saying should be understood as a statement of protest: Jesus complaining that "the manner of his arrest . . . misrepresents his character" (Nineham 1963: 396). Nevertheless, the words also resonate with Jesus' saying about the thief who binds the strong man (Mark 3: 27). During Jesus' arrest, an unnamed follower of his draws a sword and violently attacks a member of the arresting group (Mark 14: 47). Would this happen if Jesus and his followers were not already a violent group?

Jesus' interrogation by the high priests follows his arrest. As was noted above, this interrogation centers on the question of Jesus' identity—that is, whether or not Jesus claims to be the Christ, the son of God, the king of Israel. In other words, the violence of Jesus' arrest has a great deal to do with the kingdom of God. Jesus is eventually scourged and crucified as "the King of the Jews" (Mark 15: 26) by the Romans. He dies in the place of Barabbas, one of "the insurgents who had done murder during the uprising" (Mark 15: 7).[11] Mark's story suggests that the Romans perceive Jesus as a violent man and a political danger. Mark's entire narrative sequence from Jesus' arrest until his death is steeped in violence.

However, probably the most explicitly violent action by Jesus in the gospel of Mark is the so-called "cleansing" of the temple in chapter 11. This, along with the inflammatory parable of the vineyard discussed above, sets the stage for the violence of the passion story that follows. Immediately after his messianic entry into Jerusalem (Mark 11: 1–11), Jesus retires to Bethany. The next day he proceeds to the temple. "And he went into the temple and began to drive out those who sold and bought in the temple, and he overturned the tables of the money changers and the stalls of the sellers of doves, and he would not let anyone carry any vessel through the temple" (Mark 11: 15–16). The temple, Jesus says, has become "a den of robbers" (Mark 11: 17). This saying is reminiscent of the saying about the strong man's house in Mark 3: 27, although here too it appears to be Jesus who is the intruder. It also anticipates Jesus' own arrest later on as a "highwayman" (Mark 14: 48). In this story, not only Jesus' language but his actions are violent.

As in the vineyard parable, the gospel of Mark's story of the cleansing of the temple describes the contest of power between Jesus and the high priests and the scribes, and they respond to Jesus' violence in kind, by seeking to destroy Jesus. However, unlike the son in the vineyard parable, who is comparable to the suffering son of man described above, in this story Jesus actively interferes with the affairs of the temple. He does not simply request what he wants, but instead he aggressively seeks it out. Like the thief in the strong man saying, Jesus breaks into "the house." He is more like the apocalyptic son of man who comes with power. Nevertheless, unlike this son of man, it appears that Jesus' time has not yet come.

As Mark does on several other occasions, the story of Jesus cleansing the temple is woven into the middle of another story. This other story, the cursing of the fig tree, is also a story of Jesus' violence.

> [A]s they went out from Bethany, [Jesus] was hungry; and seeing in the distance a fig tree which had leaves, he went to see if he could find anything on it; and when he reached it he found nothing but the leaves, for it was not the season for figs. Then he spoke forth and said to it: May no one eat fruit from you any more, forever. And his disciples heard him.
>
> (Mark 11: 12–14)

Jesus curses the tree when he finds no fruit on it. This also is a story of conflict, but in this case the conflict is between Jesus' hunger and the fact that "it was not the season for figs." Jesus' curse seems childish and cruel, especially since it is miraculously effective: "As they passed by in the [next] morning they saw the fig tree dried up, from the roots; and Peter remembered and said to him: Master, see, the fig tree which you cursed is dried up" (Mark 11: 20–1). The fig tree appears once more in Mark 13: 28, in Jesus' words and in an apocalyptic context: "From the fig tree learn its parable. When its branch is tender and it puts forth leaves, you know that the summer is near." This image of timeliness contrasts ironically with Jesus' untimeliness in cursing the fig tree.

Here again the tension between the uncanny and the marvelous in the identity of Jesus comes into play. The effective cursing of the tree is a marvelous deed, but of little political consequence. The cleansing of the temple is an uncanny deed of considerable political significance. In this instance, however, the tension does not concern the ambiguous identity of the son of man, but rather it concerns the meaning of Jesus' actions. By intercalating these two stories, the gospel of Mark highlights the violence at the center of each of them. Each story illuminates and "translates" the other. The unreasonableness of Jesus' violence in the temple is emphasized by the unseasonableness of his expectations from the fig tree. This suggests that Jesus' violent interference with the temple procedures is also not appropriate, at least not at this time. Reciprocally, the association of the temple with the kingdom of God (and of the priests with the tenants in the vineyard) makes Jesus' heartless attack on the tree just as much an attack on the kingdom as is his attack on the temple itself.

Each of the intercalated stories also criticizes the other. Because of its juxtaposition with the temple cleansing, the cursing of the fig tree becomes more significant and tells the reader more about the character of Jesus than it would otherwise. Conversely, the cleansing of the temple becomes *less* significant—just another violent outburst by a man who curses trees! Intercalation of stories such as this is not unusual in the gospel of Mark, which both comments on and undermines the significance of its own narratives by the ways that it weaves the stories together.

Violence, utopia and the identity of Jesus

[S]ince the convergence of the referential and the figural signification can never be established, the reference can never be a meaning . . . there is room only for "wild" connotation; the loss of denominational control means that every connotation has claim to referential authority but no statute in which to ground this claim.

(de Man 1979: 208)

The foregoing is not an exhaustive survey of Jesus' violence in the gospel of Mark. Nor are depictions of similarly violent words and actions of Jesus absent from the other biblical gospels. The gospels of Matthew and Luke both draw heavily on material from Mark, including some of the material depicting Jesus' violent words and deeds that was discussed above. Sometimes this material is largely unchanged, but sometimes it is rewritten to suit Matthew's or Luke's own distinct version of the story of Jesus.

In addition, the gospels of Matthew and Luke present a great deal of narrative material that does not appear in Mark, such as the Q saying with which I began, as well as other material unique to each of them. Many of Jesus' parables in Matthew and Luke, such as the treasure in the field (Matthew 13: 44), the net (Matthew 13: 47–50), and the good Samaritan (Luke 10: 30–7), have overtones of violence not unlike those of Mark 4: 26–9. Matthew and Luke both omit this parable of the seed growing secretly, but each of them on the whole contains more parables than Mark does. Jesus' "son of man" language with its ambiguous double focus also appears in Matthew and Luke. Jesus' verbal exchanges with his opponents, like his exorcizing of demons, are often accompanied by violent words or actions on his part in each of the synoptic gospels.

However, in the gospel of Mark the uncertainty of Jesus' identity occupies a central position that it does not have in any other biblical gospel. For example, both Matthew and Luke separate (but in different ways) the cleansing of the temple story from the cursing of the fig tree, thus eliminating Mark's ironic metatextual commentary on Jesus' (un)timeliness. Even though both Matthew and Luke contain "son of man" sayings of the two types noted above, each of them asserts more clearly in various ways that Jesus is indeed the son of man, thus resolving at least some of Mark's indeterminacies in that regard.

As was noted above, in Mark 13: 6 Jesus prophesies that "many will come in my name, saying: I am he (*egô eimi*). And they will lead many astray." In Mark 14: 62, answering the high priest's question ("are you the Christ?"), Jesus says, "I am he (*egô eimi*)." The gospel of Mark here seems to present Jesus as fulfilling his own prophecy—that is, as a "false Christ and false prophet" (Mark 13: 22) who may lead many people, including the reader, astray. The warning at Mark 13: 14 ("let him who reads this take note of it") suggests the need for cautious reading. Surely if the parable of the seed growing secretly can be read in the light of either Mark's allegorized sower parable or Matthew's apocalyptic parable of the wheat and the weeds, then this reading of Jesus as the false Christ is also possible, although probably not desirable. It may even be blasphemous (Mark 3: 28, 14: 64). The consequence of inter and intratextual reading such as this is what Paul de Man (1979) calls "the loss of denominational control."[12] Both Matthew and Luke, by clarifying Mark's ambiguous account of Jesus' answer to the high priest, eliminate the possibility of these textual juxtapositions and their blasphemous consequences.

Biblical scholars often resolve the fantastic indeterminacy of Jesus' identity in the gospel of Mark into the "messianic secret." This theory holds that according to Mark, Jesus is deliberately keeping secret the truth that he is really the Christ until an appropriate time to reveal this information. That time arrives during his interrogation by the high priest, at which point Jesus' "I am he" answer to the priest's direct question is an unequivocal affirmation of messianic identity. The messianic secret theory overcomes the ambiguities of Jesus' identity in Mark, much as the reading of the parable of the seed growing secretly in either an apocalyptic or an allegorical fashion (but not both) resolves the meaning of that parable and de-fantasizes it. The scholars' messianic secret theory eliminates the fantastic dimension of Mark's story, just as Matthew or Luke in their revisions of Mark's material also tend to eliminate the fantastic dimension.

The uncertainty of Jesus' identity is closely associated with the violence that surrounds his words and deeds. One striking feature of the characters in the gospel of Mark is their frequent response of fear or astonishment to Jesus' words and deeds. The crowds, his followers, and his opponents all respond to him in this way. The disciples are afraid: "And they were seized with a great fear and said to each other: Who is this, that the wind and sea obey him?" (Mark 4: 41) The crowd is astonished: "From where does the man derive all this, and what is this wisdom that has been given to him, and what are these powers that are fulfilled by his hands? Is not this the carpenter, the son of Mary and the brother of James and Joseph and Judas and Simon? And are not his sisters here among us?" (Mark 6: 2–3) The priests and scribes decide to arrest Jesus, but "not during the festival, for so there will be rioting among the people" (Mark 14: 2). This response of fear and astonishment point both to Jesus' violence and to the fantastic indeterminacy of his identity.

The fantastic ambiguity of Jesus' identity in the gospel of Mark makes his violence more troubling to other characters in the story— but also to the reader. Beneath the answer of "violence" to the guessing game that is the gospel of Mark lies the even deeper question of Jesus' identity. The answer to this question is not to be found even in Mark's unsaid, for it is forestalled by the fantastic elements that appear throughout Mark's story. The identity of Jesus remains not secret but uncertain throughout Mark's narrative. Is he an uncanny human being or a marvelous divine being? Is he a revolutionary or a holy man? The fantastic element in Mark's story subverts these oppositions. The indeterminacies of Mark's narrative (between "the referential and the figural signification") both provoke and resist the "wild connotations" that readers produce, such as those noted above, and many others.

In Mark, Jesus rarely speaks of the Christ. He would rather talk about the son of man.

> "And you, who do you say I am?" Peter answered and said to him: "You are the Christ." Then [Jesus] warned [*epetimêsen*, "rebuked"] them to tell no one about him. Then he began to explain to them that the son of man must suffer much.
>
> (Mark 8: 29–31)

This dialogue with the disciples should be read in conjunction with Mark 14: 61–2, Jesus' dialogue with the high priest. Both dialogues fantastically juxtapose the Christ and the son of man. (But is it the *same* son of man in each case? One suffers, and the other comes in power.) Jesus rebukes his disciples just as he rebukes the demons, or the stormy sea (Mark 4: 39). Is it because Jesus wants the truth about his identity to stay secret? Or instead, is it because he does not like Peter's answer to his question? Both Matthew and Luke significantly change Mark's dialogue between Jesus and his disciples, much as they change the dialogue with the high priest. In each case, these gospels clarify Jesus' messianic identity. In Matthew and Luke, Jesus' righteous violence is directed unambiguously against the wicked violent ones who seek to possess the kingdom of God.

In the view of J.R.R. Tolkien, fantasy requires the "subcreation" of a "secondary world" characterized by "eucatastrophe" and *evangelium* (1966: 49). However, in the gospel of Mark the conjunction of fantasy and violence does not refer to the kingdom of God as a secondary world, a place to which we escape from this one. Instead, for Mark the kingdom of God is a hermeneutical problem, which is also the problem of the identity of Jesus. Is Jesus' violence in the gospel of Mark on behalf of the kingdom of God or against it? Does Jesus defend the kingdom or does he seek to take it by force? The kingdom itself is also uncertain in Mark. Is it this-worldly or other-worldly, political or spiritual, allegorical or apocalyptic?

The kingdom of God in Mark is a site of disruption of the realistic "primary" world of conventional everyday experience, not the consoling *evangelium* of Tolkien. The fantastic subversiveness of the gospel of Mark appears at numerous points where Mark becomes difficult to read. The fantastic "identity" of the gospel of Mark, and of Jesus as a character in the gospel of Mark, is produced by frequent disruptions of reference to extratextual truth or reality. These disruptions are often generated by Jesus' words or deeds of violence in regard to the kingdom. Nevertheless, as Todorov (1973) says, the fantastic hesitation is generically unstable; it cannot be maintained. The readers cannot be satisfied with the indeterminacies in Mark's story. At these points of difficulty they are tempted to supply answers of their own, to decide the identity of Jesus or the proper reading of a parable, or to overlook the words that are there in the text, such as the coincidence of "I am" in both Mark 13: 6 and 14: 62 or the exchange of rebukes in 8: 29–33.

The gospel of Mark has always been the least popular, and the most suspect theologically, of the biblical gospels. Readers are often tempted to read Mark's difficult passages in the light of gospels such as Matthew or Luke, which often resolve the difficulties and eliminate their fantastic ambiguity. The reader's desire for narrative coherence and meaning is the desire for ideology.[13] Ideology provides each reader with a sense of identity and reality, a coherence of self and of world, that is affirmed and echoed in the story itself. Elements of the fantastic in the gospel of Mark—in this case, the twin problems of the identity of Jesus and of the nature of his relationship to the kingdom of God—attack and subvert the ideological structures that establish reality. The fantastic indeterminacies in Mark yield ideological consequences in the reader's understanding of the text.

Perhaps the time of violence of which both Matthew 11: 12–14 and Luke 16: 16 speak is a time that calls for a new scripture, a scripture that will secure the kingdom of God against the violence of its enemies. Luke 16: 16 sets the "good news" or gospel that "is announced" (in texts such as the gospels of Matthew or Luke) over against "the law and the prophets" of the Jewish scriptures. Both Matthew and Luke present themselves as expressions of the law, authoritative scriptures that will not fail (Luke 16: 17). They are the good news that brings to an end the period of violence against the kingdom. In both Matthew and Luke it is clear that Jesus is the son of man and that he stands on the side of the kingdom of God. Jesus affirms the law even as he "completes" it:

> Do not think that I have come to destroy the law and the prophets. I have not come to destroy but to complete. Indeed, I say to you, until the sky and the earth are gone, not one iota or one end of a letter must go from the law, until all is done. He who breaks one of the least of these commandments and teaches men accordingly shall be called the least in the Kingdom of Heaven; he who performs and teaches these commandments shall be called great in the Kingdom of Heaven.
>
> (Matthew 5: 17–19)

This is why Matthew 11: 12–14 and Luke 16: 16, the two versions of the saying about violence and the kingdom of God with which this essay opened, can be so explicit. They can speak openly the forbidden word, "violence," the answer to Mark's guessing game.

Notes

1 All translations from the biblical gospels are from Lattimore (1979).
2 Some commentators think that Luke's version of the saying is secondary to Matthew's version (Drury 1976: 160; Fenton 1963: 179). A similar text is saying 8 of the non-canonical gospel of the Nazoreans: "the kingdom of heaven is plundered" (Cameron 1982: 99). Another non-canonical saying of Jesus compares the kingdom to an act of extreme violence. This is saying 98 of the gospel of Thomas: "The Kingdom of the Father is like a certain man who wanted to kill a powerful man. In his own house he drew his sword and stuck it into the wall in order to find out whether his hand could carry through. Then he slew the powerful man" (Cameron 1982: 35).
3 "This pericope is a notorious *crux interpretum* and virtually every detail is disputed: its position in the order of Q, the original order of its two component statements (Matthew 11: 12–13; Luke 16: 16a, b), the reconstruction of the original saying and its meaning" (Kloppenborg 1987: 113).
4 "Violence" is, of course, only one of many words that does not occur in Mark. "Kingdom" (Greek *basileia*) does appear in Mark, but this word is relatively rare there, as compared to the other synoptic gospels (twenty times in Mark, fifty-five times in Matthew, forty-six times in Luke).
5 However, Nineham claims that "the strong one" might have been an early Christian term for Jesus (1963: 120) (see also Taylor 1953: 241). The lack of any narrative context for the parallel version in saying 35 of the gospel of Thomas (Cameron 1982: 29) leaves the identities of both the strong man and the thief quite unclear in that saying. Comparison of these two versions of the saying make clear how important the larger textual context is in the reader's construction of meaning.
6 See Taylor 1953: 265–6.
7 *Ôdinôn*, Mark 13: 8—"the agony" according to Lattimore (1979); "the birth-pangs" according to the Revised Standard Version. In a different context, but perhaps with a similar result, is the saying of Jesus that commends violence against oneself: "if your hand makes you go amiss, cut it off; it is better for you to go into life one-handed than with both hands to wander off into Gehenna, into the quenchless fire. And if your foot makes you go amiss, cut it off; it is better for you to go into life lame than with both feet to be thrown into Gehenna. And if your eye makes you go amiss, pluck it out; it is better for you to go one-eyed into the Kingdom of God than with both eyes to be thrown into Gehenna, where their worm does not die and the fire is not quenched" (Mark 9: 43–8).
8 See also Aichele (1996): 106ff.
9 I consider Mark to end at 16: 8.
10 Nineham notes that *lêstên* ("highwayman") can also be translated as "insurrectionist" (1963: 396); see also Bauer (1957), *lêstês*, as well as the following note.
11 In a variant on the parallel to this verse in Matthew 27: 16, Barabbas' first name is given as "Jesus." "Barabbas" means "son of the father (*abba*)." Jesus prays to "Abba, Father" in Mark 14: 36. Does Jesus the son

of Abba die so that Jesus the son of Abba may be freed? See Aichele (1996): 13ff.

12 De Man argues throughout many of his writings that this loss occurs in *all* readings.

13 This point is developed more fully in Aichele (1996), especially chapters 6 and 7.

6

BLASPHEMY AND THE RECOVERY OF THE SACRED

Gene Doty

God casts a long shadow

In a pair of novels, *Black Easter* ([1969] 1982a) and *The Day After Judgment* ([1971] 1982b), James Blish tells a story that ends with God's death and Satan sitting on God's throne. The other two novels discussed here portray this conflict between God and Satan with more conventional results than Blish's. These novels, *This Present Darkness* (1986) by Frank Peretti and *That Hideous Strength* (1965b), by C.S. Lewis, have similar plots involving satanic conspiracies. Both Lewis and Peretti conclude their books with the triumph of God's side, rather than his enemy's. Although differing in theology (as well as literary skills), Lewis and Peretti wrote as Christians, while Blish wrote as an agnostic (Stableford 1979: 54) using the trappings of Christian eschatology and ceremonial magic to explore the relationships between the divine and the devilish.

For pious readers the outcome of Blish's novels is at least shocking and probably blasphemous. The Western concept of blasphemy rests on a strict dualism that divides God as absolutely good from Satan as absolutely evil,[1] just as the Western myth of Satan presents him as God's enemy, determined against all odds to occupy the divine throne. As Jeffrey Burton Russell says in *Satan: The Early Christian Tradition*, "the conflict between good and evil stands at the center of Christianity" (1981: 227). Blasphemy involves an opposition—not between the sacred and the secular—but between the sacred and the profane. Strictly speaking, a secular attitude is not blasphemous. In order to blaspheme, one must accept the sacred view of the universe and oppose the good. Thus, the agnostic Blish necessarily uses a sacred worldview as the context for *Black Easter* ([1969] 1982a) and *The Day After Judgment* ([1971] 1982b).

According to Russell, the Christian conception of God as perfectly and exclusively good creates a need for an anti-God: an original, unitary godhead, encompassing both good and evil, has been split into "the good Lord and the evil Devil" (Russell 1981: 228). In psychological terms, the devil becomes "the shadow side of God" (1981: 251). Because the dualistic God is incomplete, the human need for wholeness can lead to experiencing the devil as sacred, as "negatively numinous" (Otto 1958: 106–7, note). The theological dualism is brought inside the human psyche, which is then split against itself.

For Otto, the dark and fearful numinous is an intrinsic part of the human experience of the holy. Popular Christianity's absolute dualism makes only half of the holy available, the other half being the evil Other, God's shadow. Similarly, Jungian psychology posits integration of the "shadow" aspect of the personality as the first step in healing (von Franz 1964: 168–76).

In the Christian myth, this tension between good and evil is resolved eschatologically, by a final battle between God and the devil. Apocalyptic portions of the Bible, such as Daniel and Revelation, describe history as ending with an ultimate conflict between good and evil. In this conflict, the devil attempts to displace God through his tool, the Antichrist.

For instance, the Beast of Revelation, chapter 13, both blasphemes against God and makes war against the saints (verses 5–7). Along with such passages as Paul's warnings against the "lawless one" (2 Thessalonians 2: 3–4), this vision of a blasphemous counterpart to God, involved in a cosmic conflict, provides a dramatic situation for authors of fantastic literature. The apocalyptic imagery of the final battle between good and evil involves humans, animals, the elements of nature, and unnatural monsters. It could be argued that one of the enduring appeals of the book of Revelation is to the human taste for the fantastic. And, beyond the obvious appeal of dramatic and bizarre imagery, there is the underlying psychological attraction of the conflict of opposites.

The novels under discussion all use theological and psychological dualism as the framework for their plots. Frank Peretti and C.S. Lewis resolve the conflict with the victory of God over the blasphemous opposition. This resolution leaves the theological and psychological dualism intact. Real wholeness can only come about by transcending the terms of the dualism. Only James Blish's novels offer such a transcendence of the divided opposites and thus depict a situation in which humans experience all the dimensions of the holy as described by Otto. For that reason, this chapter emphasizes Blish's work, using Peretti's and Lewis' novels to provide a contrasting context.

Demons cast human shadows

Frank Peretti's novel, *This Present Darkness* (1986), uses the imagery of biblical Apocalypse quite literally to plot a fundamentalist response to currently popular horror fiction. This popular novel has sold over one million copies (Miller 1990: 88). In *This Present Darkness*, a small college town, Ashton, is attacked by demons using "New Age" ideas as a cover. The demonic New Age conspiracy is opposed by Hank Busche, a "praying pastor," and Marshall Hogan, a skeptical newspaper editor who has a jailhouse conversion. Unseen by the human characters, numerous angels and demons act behind the scenes, protecting, attacking, and guiding the humans on their respective sides of the war. Since Peretti's position is pure fundamentalist Christianity, the outcome of the war is assured in advance.

This Present Darkness begs to be compared with the novels of C.S. Lewis, Charles Williams, and even J.R.R. Tolkien. In comparison with these major works of Christian fantasy, it comes off very poorly. The characters are unconvincing, the depictions of angels and demons use the same stereotyped imagery repeatedly, and the human characters all seem to be puppets manipulated either by angels or demons. There is nothing in the book to suggest why one would be a Christian, except to escape the demons' assaults. Peretti's negative reason for conversion to Christianity pales besides Lewis' positive vision of the Tao, as discussed below.

Two descriptions of demonic assault display the limited range of Peretti's portrayal of these creatures. Early in the novel, a minor demon is pursuing the newspaper editor, Marshall Hogan:

> Unseen by Marshall, small wisps of sulfurous breath crept along the floor like slow water, along with an unheard scraping and scratching over the tiles. Like a slimy black leech, the little demon clung to him, its taloned fingers entwining Marshall's legs . . . , poisoning his spirit.
>
> (Peretti 1986: 39)

Sandy, Marshall Hogan's daughter, gets involved with the satanists without realizing what they are. Having been taught to meditate,

Sandy meets a beautiful spirit being who befriends her. Later, Sandy gets her first real sight of this being whom she has considered benevolent: "Her [the being's] hide was soot-black and leathery. Her eyes were huge yellow orbs" (Peretti 1986: 355). With a few minor variations, all the demons are described in these simplistic terms.

Descriptions of angels are equally stereotyped; with the exception of Betsy, "a perfect farmer's daughter" (Peretti 1986: 300), Peretti's angels are "strongly built, perfectly proportioned" males (Peretti 1986: 9). Just like the demons, the angels guide the thoughts and actions of humans. Angelic manipulation of the human characters is seen most clearly when the leader of the angelic hosts says that both Hogan and Busche must be sacrificed "for a season" (Peretti 1986: 200); throughout the book, both angels and demons control humans for their own reasons, without the humans quite knowing what is going on.

Marshall Hogan becomes a Christian while in jail. The moment of his conversion is expressed in the dualistic terms endemic in fundamentalism: He says to the preacher, Hank Busche, who is his cellmate, "Hank, I'm just no good. I need God. I need Jesus" (Peretti 1986: 316). Compared with Mark Studdock's conversion in *That Hideous Strength* (Lewis 1965b, discussed below), Marshall Hogan's accepting Jesus is flat and undramatic. Further, Marshall places his natural self on the side of evil— "I'm just no good"—while locating all good on God's side of the division. For the fundamentalist, what is merely human can only be allied with the devil.

This Present Darkness and its sequels are popular with conservative Christians. The demonic conspiracy embodies a comprehensive range of fundamentalist enemies, including moral relativism (Peretti 1986: 35), religious tolerance (1986: 75), intellectualism and psychology (1986: 37), liberal Christian theology (1986: 65), hypnotism (1986: 78), neopaganism (1986: 91), mysticism, meditation and higher consciousness (1986: 109), and even the lotus position (1986: 217), which Peretti shows as leading to demonic possession.[2] In *This Present Darkness* the opposition between faith and blasphemy is clearly drawn: "blasphemy" means opposition to God through advocacy of all the things that fundamentalists oppose.

The strongest feature of *This Present Darkness* is its plot. Peretti explains that he took great care in graphing the plot of the book before writing it (Miller 1990: 97). He obviously did his job well. As weak as characterization and other aspects of the book might be, the movement of the great abstractions in conflict appeals to the inherent dualism of our culture. Written without subtlety, *This*

Present Darkness still grips the reader with the starkness of its conflict.

The normal casts crooked shadows

This Present Darkness resembles C.S. Lewis' *That Hideous Strength* (1965b) in many ways, the basic resemblance being the demonic plot masquerading as a harmless educational endeavor. Peretti's novel lacks the depth and resonance of Lewis'; where Peretti uses caricatures and stereotypes, Lewis develops at least his main characters with more subtlety. More important, for this discussion, Lewis has a subtler conception of blasphemy and the spiritual forces involved than does Peretti.

In order to discuss, *That Hideous Strength* I will look first at Lewis' book on education, *The Abolition of Man* (1965a), which suggests a more comprehensive definition of blasphemy than presented so far. In this book, Lewis uses the Chinese term, Tao, or Way, to express the universal belief in an inherent pattern in nature. Lewis defines the Tao as "reality beyond all predicates," "the Way in which the universe goes on," "which every man should tread in imitation" (Lewis 1965a: 28). Since the Tao is seen as the model for human action, the possibility of departing from the model arises.

Not only might one depart from the Tao inadvertently, but one might also deliberately oppose the "Way of Nature." For C.S. Lewis, opposition to nature *is* opposition to God, since God is the creator of Nature. For Lewis, blasphemy can be seen as distortion or inversion of the "normal;" in this perspective, it does not have to do so much with morals as with pattern, with what is "right" in the old sense of "straight" versus crooked, of what is on target versus what is astray or askew. For Lewis, following the good and having faith in God are a consequence of the "normal."

In *That Hideous Strength*, the third novel of his space trilogy, Lewis combines the notion of the anti-natural with the blasphemous. In the book, a small British university town is threatened by a research institution known as the NICE—the National Institute for Coordinated Experiments. While posing as an advanced scientific project, the NICE is actually a front for an inner circle which is consorting with demons. By resuscitating the head of an executed criminal, the conspirators hope to provide a means for Satan to exercise direct control on earth.

Reflecting Lewis' position in *The Abolition of Man*, the NICE's opposition to God is also an opposition to God's creation. The NICE disrupts the normal lives of the people around it, using both humans and animals for experiments. Fittingly, the criminal's head is destroyed by a bear on which the NICE had intended to experiment.

Contrary to Peretti, Lewis does not present the demonic directly. Instead, he relies on suggestion, tone, and human proxies. The deputy director of the NICE, a man named Wither, reduces Mark Studdock to helpless confusion by refusing to answer questions directly, by appearing absent-minded, by speaking "vaguely and alarmingly" of things that perturb Studdock (Lewis 1965b: 119). When Wither and two close associates appear before the demonic head, Lewis' description emphasizes the grotesqueness and obscenity of the three men, who assault each other before the head, rather than providing details of the head itself (Lewis 1965b: 354–5).

Mark Studdock is the human protagonist of the book; he is a young academic, a sociologist, who is both ambitious and insecure. Studdock is exposed to blasphemous opposition to nature (or to the Tao) in the scene where the NICE attempts to brainwash him. It does this by subjecting him to a perceptually distorted room and surrealistic pictures. The effect is an assault on the reason: "Every fold of drapery, every piece of architecture, had a meaning one could not grasp but which withered the mind" (Lewis 1965b: 299). Quite against the intentions of those who designed it, the room's effect on Studdock is to convert him to the "normal" and, ultimately, to God. As Studdock's vision of the world shifts, Lewis says, "there rose up against this background of the sour and the crooked some kind of vision of the sweet and the straight . . . something he vaguely called the 'Normal'" (Lewis 1965b: 299). The "Normal" which Mark Studdock envisions here is the Tao of Lewis' *The Abolition of Man*, and perceiving it is Studdock's first step towards faith in God.

In contrast with Marshall Hogan's conversion, Mark Studdock's is much more convincing because the reader gets to know Studdock much better, and Lewis' psychology is more realistic and convincing. In essence, however, both Hogan and Studdock have chosen allegiance with the Good over Evil in a dualistic context. Even given Lewis' sophistication, the normal is irreconcilable with the crooked in *That Hideous Strength*.

Blasphemy casts a sacred shadow

James Blish's *Black Easter* ([1969] 1982a) and *The Day After Judgment* ([1971] 1982b) are part of a trilogy with the overall title, *After Such Knowledge* (1991). Brian Stableford (1979) says *After Such Knowledge* is

Blish's "major contribution to modern literature" (1979: 52). This trilogy actually consists of four separately published novels (in order of publication): *A Case of Conscience* ([1959] 1991), *Doctor Mirabilis* ([1964] 1991), *Black Easter* ([1968] 1982a), and *The Day After Judgment* ([1971] 1982b). The first novel is science fiction, the second historical fiction, and the last two fantasy. This mixed-genre trilogy was published in one volume only after Blish's death (1991) and has yet to receive the attention it deserves. Only the first book, *A Case of Conscience*, is well-known. The last two titles, published separately, encompass a single plot and may be referred to as a "dyptich" (Ketterer 1987: 309).

This dyptich, *Black Easter* and *The Day After Judgment* (recently reissued as *Devil's Day*, 1990) presents a radically blasphemous version of the Christian eschatological myth. The plot of *Black Easter* and *The Day After Judgment* reflects Lewis' plot in *That Hideous Strength* as there is an effort to release demons on the earth (*Black Easter* is dedicated to Lewis' memory).

As noted earlier, while both Peretti and Lewis wrote as believing Christians, Blish wrote as an agnostic. Rather than a theological eschatology, he held to a Spenglerian view of history, as expressed in his essay, "Probapossible Prolegomena to Idereal History" (1987). In this essay, Blish describes the last phase of a civilization's life-cycle, which he sees as the current phase of our own civilization: there comes to be a "'second religiousness' in which no one actually believes" and science and occultism are intermingled (Blish 1987: 79). David Ketterer's discussion (1987: 313–15) clearly draws the connections between Blish's essay and *Black Easter* and *The Day After Judgment*; the point here is that, even as an agnostic, Blish held to a view of history in which a civilization's existence ended in decline, chaos, and occult activity. Blish's view resembles Peretti's and Lewis' Christian eschatology in this basic structure of a decline into scientistic occultism and violence. For this reason, Blish could easily adapt Christian eschatology and Western demonology to his purposes.

Writing as William Atheling, Jr, Blish commented on *That Hideous Strength* (Lewis 1965b) that it expresses "a chiliastic crisis"—a period when humans expect the Apocalypse but do not believe in divine forgiveness (Blish 1964: 54). This description fits *Black Easter* and *The Day After Judgment* perfectly, aligning them with the concerns of Christian novelists like Lewis and Peretti. A comment of Thomas J.J. Altizer's is pertinent here: discussing James Joyce, Altizer asserts that the blasphemous aspects of Joyce's writing were necessary, because in a time of insincere religion, blasphemy becomes "the major mode of religious speech" (1985: 210). Altizer's comment on Joyce is especially relevant to Blish because of Blish's strong interest in Joyce (Ketterer 1987: 23). Unlike Peretti and Lewis, Blish is willing to use blasphemy as a "mode of religious speech" and follow it through to its conclusion, which transcends the enmity of God and Satan.

In *Black Easter* ([1968] 1982a), a weapons manufacturer named Baines engages a magician, Theron Ware, to set free as many demons as possible on the world for a limited time to "'see just what it is they would do if they were left on their own hooks like that'" (Blish [1968] 1982a: 108). Baines has become bored with the possibilities of "natural" destruction, and wants to release the demons to relieve his boredom. Baines embodies Mircea Eliade's point, in *The Sacred and the Profane* (1959), that the secular person is not free of myth or religion, but can be subject to "hybrid forms of black magic and sheer travesty of religion" (1959: 205–6). And, of course, Baines' dabbling in the occult reflects the last phase of a civilization as described by Blish in "Probapossible Prolegomena to Idereal History" (1987).

Blish describes the demons summoned by Ware in vivid detail, using the trappings of Western ceremonial magic. The demons appear in a wide variety of uncanny and grotesque appearances. One example is "Baal, great king and commander in the East, of the order of the Fly." Baal appears as "a thing like a man, in a new surcoat and snow-white linen, but with two supernumerary heads, the one on the left like a toad's, the one on the right like a cat's" (Blish [1968] 1982a: 140–1). The procession of demons leaves the reader exhausted and unsettled. Their astounding energy and variety both entertain and threaten. Peretti's demons seem petty and weak by comparison. Lewis' evil characters, on the other hand, are all too human in their frightening commitment to evil and chaos.

Eliade posits a basic human need for the sacred: "Man desires to recover the active presence of the gods" (Eliade 1959: 98). In *Black Easter*, Baines begins as a secular man but enters the realm of the sacred through his initiation by Ware. Eliade says flatly, "Life is not possible without an opening towards the transcendent," and he points out that the sacred may be experienced via the underworld as well as through the heavens (Eliade 1959: 34). Baines' experience, as much as Studdock's in *That Hideous Strength*, falls within the realm of the sacred, even though Baines experiences the sacred only through demons, whereas Studdock rejects the negatively numinous to embrace the normal.

The other two main characters in *Black Easter* and *Day After*

Judgment are the magician, Theron Ware, and a Catholic priest, Father Domenico. (Another significant character is Baines' special assistant, Jack Ginsberg.) Both Ware and Father Domenico are concerned that Baines' project will have unforeseen effects, but Ware is certain that it will not bring about Armageddon, since "Armageddon requires the prior appearance of the Antichrist" (Blish [1968] 1982a: 109), and Ware does not believe that that figure is yet in the world.

It is notable that Ware follows the traditional depiction of events accompanying Armageddon; the world of *Black Easter* and *The Day After Judgment* reflects fundamentalist interpretations of the Bible combined with Western ceremonial magic (Ketterer 1987: 297–8). However, Blish turns the biblical imagery upside down to confront the reader with a vision in which Baines' Faustian experiment goes out of control and the demons take over, causing massive destruction. The words of Nietzsche's Zarathustra have come true: Zarathustra's proclamation, "God is dead," is the last sentence of *Black Easter*.

In *The Sacred and the Profane,* Eliade shows that in mythical thinking, chaos and disintegration precede a new creation (1959: 131). In a section entitled "Regeneration Through Return to the Time of Origins," Eliade discusses the way in which archaic healing rituals involve a return to the time of creation: "life cannot be repaired, it can only be recreated through symbolic repetition of the cosmogony" (Eliade 1959: 82).

In Western culture's basic mythology, derived from the Bible, destruction—a return to chaos—is a necessary prelude to recreation.[3] Consider, for instance, the parallel between the formless void of water in the first creation narrative in Genesis and the flood that obliterates the earth a few chapters later. Further, consider the cosmic catastrophes which, in the Revelation to John, precede the "new heaven and new earth." Put formulaically, existing structures must be reduced to chaos in order to be renewed.

Lewis' *That Hideous Strength* and Peretti's *This Present Darkness* lack a thorough return to chaos; thus their renewal is partial, a conservative return to a previous condition—belief in the biblical God. In *Black Easter* and *The Day After Judgment*, however, we have a renewal in which a thorough return to chaos is followed by the most radical change imaginable. At the end of *The Day After Judgment*, Satan takes on God's role. Baines, Ware, Father Domenico and Jack Ginsberg have traveled to the City of Dis (which has surfaced in Death Valley). There they have an audience with Satan, who, in Miltonic blank verse, expresses a non-dualist view of good and evil:

> Good is independent, but the bad
> Cannot alone survive;
>   . . .
> for the Good is free
> To act or not, while evill hath been will'd
> Insensate and compulsive to bring Good
> Still greater heights unto.
>
> (Blish [1971] 1982b: 159)

Satan's speech expresses an orthodox monotheistic viewpoint—only good is ultimate and independent; evil depends on good for its existence (Pagels 1995: 182). But as Pagels goes on to say, historically, many supposedly monotheistic Christians have actually held to a dualistic belief that makes evil the ontological equal of good—or have conceived of God and Satan as equal opposing powers. Both Peretti's and Lewis' novels seem to express this dualism.

In the speech quoted previously, Satan expresses agnosticism as the ultimate fate of deity, but goes on to say, "Though God/Be dead, His Throne remains" (Blish [1971] 1982b: 160), and since that throne must be filled, Satan finds that he, reluctantly, must become God. Stating that the divine had always intended for humans to become God, Satan ends his speech with a lament, "I never wanted to be God at all; 'And so, by winning all, All have I lost'" (Blish [1971] 1982b: 162). Ironically, after winning his war against God, Satan finds he must assume the role of his vanquished enemy.

After Satan's Miltonic speech, referred to above, the infernal city disappears, leaving Baines, Ware, Father Domenico, and Jack Ginsberg standing in the desert. The men are struck with wonder and barely able to speak. Each of them begins to speak but cannot complete his sentence:

Father Domenico: I think. . . .
Baines: I believe. . . .
Ware: I hope. . . .
Ginsberg: I . . . love.

> (Blish [1971] 1982b: 163–4)

These characters have resolved their doubts and inner conflicts in wonder, an essential aspect of the experience of the numinous, as described by Rudolph Otto (1958). The irony is that Baines and his companions have experienced the numinous through facing Satan and have been restored by that experience. Their incomplete sentences express their inability to put that experience into words.

The sacred casts an ironic shadow

Readers of *This Present Darkness*, *That Hideous Strength*, *Black Easter* and *The Day After Judgment* experience the interplay of the sacred and the profane within the realm of the numinous. Each author provides a different resolution to the conflict of good and evil. Both C.S. Lewis' and Frank Peretti's resolutions remain dualistic. In *This Present Darkness* and *That Hideous Strength*, good wins the battle, but the war is not over. In each case, the readers are left with a need to align themselves with one of the two sides. Lewis' resolution is more effective, since the reader can believe that Studdock is really tempted by the NICE. Peretti's resolution is less satisfactory, since there is no change in the character of Hank Busche, and Marshall Hogan's conversion is superficial.

In Blish's *Black Easter* and *The Day After Judgment*, the triumph of Satan shows how the experience of the blasphemous can transcend the division between God and Satan. Readers of *Black Easter* and *The Day After Judgment* experience the ultimate horror of the dualistic myth, the victory of Satan, followed by the dissolution of the dualism. Blish leaves the reader with a vision of a universe that "requires/That all things changing must tend t'ward [God's] state" ([1971] 1982b: 161). Blish's dyptich indicates that, for secular humanity, blasphemy can reinstate the sacred as a viable experience, as shown when the arms-maker Baines comes to faith in the supernatural through direct experience of the blasphemous. In his discussion of Joyce, Altizer says, "a sacred or primordial presence can be actual and real in our world only by way of a violent and total inversion" (1985: 241). Of the novels discussed here, only Blish's achieve this violent inversion. Rather than the partial victory of one side of a dualism, as in *This Present Darkness* and *That Hideous Strength*, Blish's vision reveals a reconciliation of opposites and a return to an integral experience of the holy, in which both the terrifying and the comforting are part of the experience of the holy.

Of course, since Blish wrote as an agnostic, the return to the holy he presents is ironic, distanced from the kind of literalism that underpins Peretti's novel. As an agnostic, Blish is not recommending a literal turn to Satanism, in contrast to Peretti and Lewis, each of whom would hope their readers arrive at "truth" through the fictions that clothe it. Blish's agnosticism and irony lay a different claim on the reader: to penetrate the fragmentary last statements of the four characters left alone in Death Valley, abandoned both by God and his satanic replacement.

Notes

1 Blasphemy, as a concept, seems limited to Western, book-centered religions—Christianity, Judaism, and Islam. According to the *Encyclopedia of Religion and Ethics*, blasphemy as a sin and ecclesiastical offense is peculiar to monotheism (669). In contrast to monotheism, among the pagan Greeks and Romans, blasphemy was considered a political crime—an offense against the state—rather than a sin (669–70). A more extreme contrast may be seen in the Zen story in which a disciple asks his master, "What is the Buddha?" The master answers, "Dried dung!" Rather than being a sacrilege, this answer is an index of the master's enlightenment (Reps 1961: 106).

2 On 23 July 1992, Charter Hospital of Columbia, Missouri sponsored a workshop on Satanism and psychiatry. The presenters were Bart Larsen, the hospital's chaplain, and Wendell Amstutz, a psychologist and founder and executive director of the National Counseling Resource Center, an anti-cult organization. Although both presenters tried hard to avoid religious statements in the workshop, they were clearly coming from a conservative Christian perspective, similar to that in *This Present Darkness*. Typically, a chart in the booklet distributed at the workshop shows links between the New Age, witchcraft, and Satanism—the links which Peretti assumes in his fictional tract.

3 This pattern is also found in Hindu mythology. A recent article in *Yoga International* details the catastrophes that accompany the transition from an age of destruction, the Kali Yuga, to an age of perfection, the Satya Yuga (Tigunait 1996). These details sound a lot like those in Christian myth—corrupt government, sexual license, false religion. Significantly, the subsequent issue printed letters from readers arguing with the details of the article's description, reminiscent of the squabbles over prophecy that are endemic to fundamentalist Christianity.

7

IMAGINING THE FUTURE-POSSIBLE

William G. Doty

A utopian prediction in 1981 that within four years "we should be able to transmit humans around the globe by radio scanning or an equivalently unexpected means" (Fuller 1981)[1] seemed to reach beyond science projection to science fiction. Yet that very prediction was only part of Buckminster Fuller's extensive efforts to imagine the world's future positively, to project scientifically informed fantasies, *fictive visions*, about the possible futures that may await us.

As we approach another millennium in 2001, such imaginative projecting seems crucial if we are to discern the metaphors and concepts that will carry us into what will surely be entirely new modes of experiencing our own planet, and perhaps others as well. Imaginative, fictive projections work by developing metaphoric appropriations of possibilities that have not yet been made operational. As artworks, they provide a malleable font of concretizations, enabling us to evaluate alternatives in advance of their social reality. J.G. Ballard's violent car crash sex novel, *Crash* (1973), found its incarnation in film (*ihre Inszenierung* in German) nearly twenty-five years later in David Cronenberg's "most controversial film of 1996" (Kenny 1997: 67) of the same name: merely a quarter of a century time-lapse between the scenes set by the master fantasist Ballard, and Cronenberg's movie scenes (see Acker 1996: 10–11).

Violence, sexuality, the Apocalypse, utopia, even postmodern non-Kingdoms of (?) G/god/s: we must be wary of drawing together too quickly the parameters of socially relevant discourse, in our late twentieth-century weariness. For the personal and social self, fictive and mythic materials provide means of imagining-before-embodying, of allowing the changing self to project possible enactments without having to live them through concretely and historically. Hence the disciplined developments of imaginative projections and fantasies of future-possibles are emotional, and intellectual, as well as ethical assignments we should not take lightly. Not many of us will have the background to elaborate or evaluate such global models as Fuller's, or such fabulous scenes as Ballard's (see W.G. Doty 1991, 1992) but *imaginal training* is a long neglected discipline we would do well to revive. Such psychic athletics would involve not so much creativity workshops or classroom study of the visual arts, as sustained attention to the full spectrum of human imaginative fictions. Such a spectrum spans from the realms of scientific data to what is usually identified as scifi/speculative or science fiction/fantasy literature—I abbreviate it here with the portmanteau SF, and advocate its relevance as an alternative voicing of all so relevant "beyond the fringe" explorations in the late twentieth-century sciences and humanities.

After preliminary remarks on some aspects of SF, I turn to the striking resemblances between conceptualizations of the mind–body relationship found in SF and in Hellenistic gnosticism.[2]

Pointing to SF and fantasy imaginings of superenhanced minds leads to consideration of some other imaginings of our possibilities for life in the future. They entail fantastic elements in reconstructions of the past as well as in constructs of the future, and may facilitate reconsideration of the dominant modern views of the individual self. Eschatological anticipations can be either negatively apocalyptic or positively hopeful, and I suggest that SF represents a strong affirmation of the human possibilities of the future, similar to Fuller's understanding that a deity "seems to wish Earthian humans to survive" no less than to William Faulkner's belief that "man will not merely endure: he will prevail" (in his famous 1950 Nobel Prize acceptance speech, which we wish less patriarchally oriented, in our multiculturally-aspiring era).

Placing speculative fiction

One older, but enormous, and even elegant anthology of SF novellas and stories (Healy and McComas 1975) accompanied a summer's work in the Vermont forest, providing from time to time a shift of mental gears. The anthology had the quality that sets up anticipations that the next story read will be as good as that just completed; the book provided a banquet of perspicuous intelligence mated with vivid imagination. I tire quickly of supermachines and threatening microbes, but quality SF has a way of transcending silly plots and

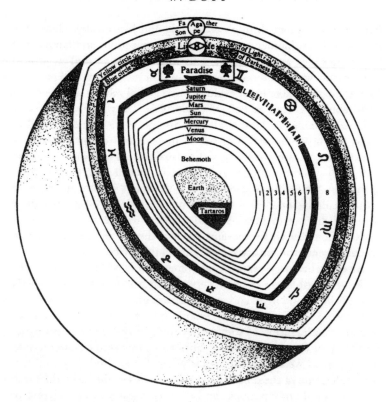

Figure 7.1 The Ophite Diagram
Source: Rudolph (1983: 68)

unlikely twelfth-hour saves by *deii ex machina*. "The good stuff" has a tensive density that generates true imaginal probes into possible alternate pasts and futures; writers such as William Gibson (*Neuromancer* 1984) even contribute new ways of conceiving possible new associations between humans and technology, or among differently gendered (Le Guin 1969, 1996) literally and imaginatively.

Such writing can be informative when it provides shapes and concretized visions of alternative directions that our culture might take, or might have taken, or might avoid. It can provide for an experimentation of the mind that does not have to subject itself to the National Bureau of the Budget, but can truly space out and embody projected societal forms in visions that more precise, demographically correct, utopias usually do not attain. Likewise, dystopian visions can

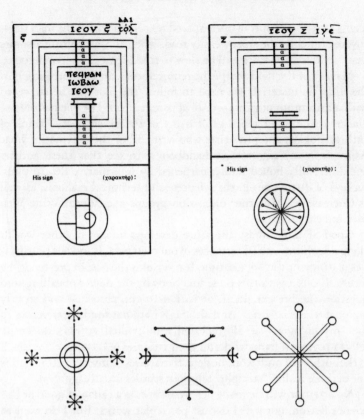

Figure 7.2 Signs (characters) and Seals of the Aeons
Source: Rudolph (1983: 174)

be studied, and specters of Orwell's *1984* (1949) come to haunt generations of its readers, in ways that careful social science talk can never engage.

Our high literary culture relegates SF *tout court* to the pulp and romances bookshelves despised by the intelligentsia. Only rarely (as in the excellent series of reprints of older classics published by Avon/Equinox as the SF Rediscovery Series) are these fictions considered more than pop culture pastimes, ephemera. And only within the past decade or so have college courses treated the genre seriously. The emerging academic respect derives from the recognition that quality SF *treats important issues*, even if in a different rhetorical mode and pace from that of traditional, reflective, social science prose. The genre seems to require a sort of open-spaced texture in which the material is covered quickly, the stories easily read, whereas high culture assumes that "serious" literature will be slow to read, dense, even ponderous.

Masters of the field accept the requirements, and it is striking how the didactic materials we need to follow the plot can be conveyed with a minimum of effort—or of apparent effort. For one has only to glance at the other writings of many of the SF authors (I think of anthropologists and physicists who write SF, or the polymathic Isaac Asimov's many informative handbooks) to see that these authors wield carefully honed tools, sharpened by informative descriptions, surveys of discoveries in the sciences, and technical manuals, as well as (increasingly) Internet discussion groups and World Wide Web lists and chat rooms.

Good SF and fantasy literature develops images of other worlds alongside those limited instances of our own past. It models possibilities of different ways of existing. It re-visions the past or pre-tends the future. It often performs these functions by the device of calling into question the present, local, or national—the parochial and strictly regional (the epichoric). And although I am not fond of references to the "mythologies" of SF, repeatedly individual authors do create religio-mythical frameworks for their trilogies or tetralogies, as much as the authors of multivolume detective stories or mysteries (but this is one of those realms "straight" religious studies usually ignores).

No attempt will be made here to delineate a canon of good or bad science fiction, nor will I discuss particular works. But I do want to reflect upon elements of the world created in SF and fantasy, and to ask what is being said about the ways our standard world concepts have been constructed. I want to highlight some of the themes that appear; to mark out some of the recurring questions, especially those focused upon the nature of personhood and the social order; and subsequently to suggest that this literature ought to be more fully integrated into the subject matter of reflective or imaginative fiction and social criticism—even, perhaps, theological reflection.

Gnostic mentations

I find it striking that so many SF stories treat some aspect of mental telepathy or advances in the technical deployment or amplification of the human mind (see Schusser 1987). Examples include the themes of disembodied mental impulses that are no longer subject to gravity, or metamorphosed humanoids whose supersensitive crania are larger than our own mammalian torsos.

Negatively, such themes reflect the sempiternal *discomfort with the flesh*, as in the gnostic conviction that in primordial times the original mindsparks were engulfed by matter, and thence transported "down" to this temporal, earthly (and inferior) existence. Such a "fall" leads in SF, as it did in the history of religious thought, to the familiar ethical dichotomy between libertine and ascetic forms of gnosticism. According to some branches, the flesh was conceived of as being so meaningless that it could be totally indulged, and hence the libertine could do anything desired, knowing one's *essential* reality to be mind, spirit. On the other hand, for the ascetic the articulated dangers of the flesh could be countered only by rigid exclusion of bodily conscious-ness. The ascetic alternative reflects less confidence in the powers and resources of the mind, perceiving it to be all too readily overpowered by the body.

Just how much the general interest in space flight in our time is motivated by similar animosity towards the "dragging" experience of earthy flesh is an open question, but often repeated SF narratives featuring suspended animation may well reflect dissatisfaction with the anthropoid corpus itself (oddly enough, this occurs in a period of absolute model tyranny of the svelte young body (see W.G. Doty 1996 and 1998);so great a tyranny that surveys repeatedly find that sixty to eighty percent of people are unhappy with their bodies, and seek to alter them quite radically). What greater control of mind over body than to treat the body as an efficient machine that can be turned off and on at will? (Char Davies, the Canadian designer of the virtual reality (VR) artwork *Osmose*, reacts quite explicitly to the usual VR "repudiation of the body," the "almost pathological denial of our materiality and mortality" (see Wertheim 1996: 30.)

The whole phenomenon of weightlessness that fascinates both SF authors and reporters of twentieth-century astronaut training programs, or the fanatic dedication to staffing extraterrestrial vehicles with supremely healthy human crew members—mere sniffles may disqualify an astronaut—further portrays a determination not to allow normal somatic functioning to run its usual course.[3] Leaving earth behind, transcending physical limitations, computer banks carrying the disembodied intelligence of the sleeping pilots: no wonder there are often such curious resemblances between SF book jackets and first-century diagrams of gnostic cosmology (see Appendix II). Two thousand years have passed, only to be a tiny step closer to the same drama of floating without penalty in freefall through the circumferential spheres![4] While NASA and likewise "spacey" religious studies/humanities forays into the frontiers of human semiotics and meanings are articulated in mass media accounts, all along, various phenomenologists have been charting in their own aesthetico-philosophical manner, some of the many relevant issues (see Bachelard 1964a, 1964b; Casey 1993).

Toward an imaginal education

Additional gnostic or hermetic themes surface in the motif of the underground, secret society or race that has kept alive true knowledge—often including "white magic"—across generations of human history (as witnessed by the extended *Dune* series by Frank Herbert 1965), and in the theme of automatic servomechanisms ("robots") that threateningly replace expensive and accident-prone human workers. In both instances, superminds must be developed and employed for administrative directivities (not just directors or directions, but virtual reality devices, entirely electronic). No one who has carried substantial administrative responsibilities can deny the appeal of such "magic" in terms of contemporary expediencies, nor have the advertisers for computer products failed to capitalize on such appeal. One advertisement for a laptop showed it being held out by two cosmic hands, lustrous rays of a nimbus streaming from around it the way such rays used to stream from representations of deities or saints; the relationship between hyperspace and the realm of the angels becomes less, rather than more, clearly understood.

I am more interested in the positive than in the negative uses of the theme of superminds, since the anti-historical gnostic tenets are as easily refuted today as they were in the Roman Empire and early Catholicism (with important exceptions such as the March 1997 suicides of the Heaven's Gate followers). Pantemporal "knowing"/ *gnosis* is hardly relevant to the ineluctably historical and specific crises of contemporary existence. But it is striking that today, except in good SF projections, theories of the potential developments of human mind are encountered only beyond the fringes of establishment thinking and learning: in theosophy or neoshamanism, or biofeedback technology (see Barfield 1977; Csikszentmihaly 1993). And that seems a wrong, short-sighted, and insufficient manner in which to treat the vast ranges of the human mind's potential. Whether or not one wishes to work from a theory of the evolving capacity of the mind, it is at least clear that we know enough about mental conditioning—about, for instance, the ways propaganda images can shape one country's experience of another—to bring some of that knowledge to bear upon the shaping of our imaginal capabilities

(Kinser and Kleinman 1969; Keen 1986; Girling 1993, are excellent accounts of how mythic perspectives impact politics).

The issue is largely one of *imaginal education*, a moral issue involving the focusing of the potent resources of our culture towards fresher and more holistic visions. In referring to the imaginal, my interest is not merely something like, "we need better art appreciation classes in high school," for all the relevance and appropriateness of that claim. I focus here not upon the appreciation and cherishing of humankind's imaginal *past*, so much as upon the ways we imagine *now*, and the ways we can learn to imagine *prospectively*, as important components within our own era, of the significantly imaginal metaphors through which succeeding generations will experience the planet's history.

Thoreau's journal entry for 6 August 1841 (Stapleton 1960) reflects his own understanding of the interlocking of past, present, and future, and I find it a helpful model: "Critical acumen is exerted in vain to uncover the past; the *past* cannot be *presented*; we cannot know what we are not. But one veil hangs over past, present, and future, and it is the province of the historian to find out, not what was, but what is" (Stapleton 1960: 7). Although our academic disciplines seem determined to separate fiction from SF, the history of thought from metafiction, retrospect and prospect, in dealing with the meaningful matters of historical, symbolic, and mythological interest, seem stubbornly joined.

I assume that is what F. Dümmler meant to indicate when he suggested that the mythographer must be a poet of theophanies as well (quoted in Palmer in his introduction to Otto 1965), the condition Mircea Eliade (1977) meant when he noted that "To the degree that you *understand* a religious fact (myth, ritual, symbol, divine figure, etc.), you *change*, you are modified" (1977: 310). Too many of our approaches to violence, utopia, and the kingdom of God have left us prospecting each such category as isolated and unique, while few of the SF devotees would accept that sort of segmentation.

The ways we usually approach the past make it merely a matter of retrospection. I remember how difficult it was for one group of students to deal with an assignment asking them to visualize their own utopian views. Mostly it was difficult because *they had none*. Apparently no one had ever sought their opinions about possible alternative pasts or futures—or more important, no one had demonstrated to them the importance of such imaginings as a creative educational act. Eventually we settled down with William Golding's *Lord of the Flies* (1954) dystopia, and slowly probed the animality of human groups, before I ventured to return to the "visualize your utopia" assignment once more. And now the proposals began to flow freely: sexuality, communications, family and school patterns, all began to be questioned and often re-imagined, re-invented, imaginatively re-conceived.

No wonder the student cry since the 1970s has been for *relevance*, for connections between that which has been, and that which may yet come to be within our own *sæculum*, our brief moment upon the limelit stage of historical significance. And no wonder our educational machinery repeatedly seems fustian, boring and stultifying. We never appreciate all the richness of the past, or learn how to make value judgments about its appropriateness, until we claim the right to utilize it in shaping fantasies for our own world and its alternatives.[5] Repeatedly in working towards greater interdisciplinary research and teaching, we hear complaints from employers that college graduates too frequently can easily amass data, but are seldom able to evaluate, integrate, and apply them. Yet we continue systematically to reward students who have trained the calculator sides of their mental equipment, and to award the significant research monies to projects that can promise arithmetically quantifiable data. The cooperative integration of the faculty–faculty or faculty–student interdisciplinary research team remains foreign to most campuses.

What if the baccalaureat were awarded only upon successful submission of an SF embodiment of the student's field of study? We are fond of being able *to make things*—note the many compounds of "to make" in everyday diction. Yet fiction, from the Latin *fingere* (*facere*), meaning literally "something made, constructed, created" (compare the cognate adjective "fictile": moldable, plastic), which should give us an opportunity to celebrate the imaginatively made, has come to carry connotations of the not made, the irreal, the unreal. Perhaps our first task ahead is to restore meaning to the full continuum of imaginal acts, emphasizing *the constructive nature of all psychomental acts and makings*, whether they be SF stories or the latest Bureau of the Census data sheets.

Every few years we hear that "the novel is dead," but the fictiveness of all imagining never becomes moribund. The supposed non-reality of the fictional must be balanced by recognition of the fictionality of all mental constructs: the fictional nature of most of the "data" and "facts" that surround us daily must be quite precisely enunciated (data is derived from *datum*, that which is "given to" us by someone; fact means literally something done or made, "factoried"). We begin to work towards such an enterprise when we make clear that even the most apparently unreal—here, SF and fantasy, but more generally all imaginative literature—is recognized as having not only sufficient daily reality to cause us to question our too easy assumptions, but indeed a surcharged reality that therapeutically extends daily realities beyond their usual limits.

Such an extension becomes indeed a propadeutics, as in Victor Turner's recommendation that the training of ethnographers should "include deriving playscripts from the best descriptive ethnographies, preferably of social dramas . . . , and encouraging the trainees to enact them, as far as possible using the symbols, speech idioms, technology, dress, insignia, and so forth, of the cultures to be visited" (1985: 223; see W.G. Doty 1990). Strangely enough few academic programs terminate with a hands-on capstone seminar integrated with the environments in which graduating students will soon find themselves working or studying.

Vibrational imaginings

Recurrently, SF suggests that persons and material objects will someday be transported across the limits of space . . . and time, although many of the novels suggest that such transmission of matter will be instantaneous. One enters the deconstruction chamber (Yale literary critics take note!) only to be reconstructed instantly in another realm, light-years distant.

Here the underlying concept respects not the usual primacy of matter or substance, but that of energy and pattern, of patterned energy, of process thought. The basic insights of atomic physics are quasi-literalized and taken beyond the deconstruction (that sounds curiously like what "narratological critics" say they are doing) to the stage of re-assemblage. Reduce the material object to its pattern of energic interactions, copy and transmit that pattern to the reconstruction chamber, and *Voila*!, a reduplicated person or object. Simultaneous resolution of two thorny problems actually facing prospects for transuniversal travel: the sheer bulk of matter, which would immobilize intra-universal vehicles, and the problem of aging in space while one endures the years of travel necessary to cross the vast distances between bodies in purely-local-cosmic dimensionalities.

And from such deconstruction-reconstruction according to patterns of energic vibration, it seems not a very large step to the relativizing of the bodily, such as we have already discovered in the gnostic parallels with SF; or to the exploration of all existence as being comprised of figments (the word is derived from our old friend *fingere*) of communally shared imaginings: the buildings, the streets, the people existing only as phantom appearances, shaped and formed in such virtual reality that they have corporeal appearances, but are essentially nothing but *vibrations*. While I know of no SF piece consciously modeled upon the Pythagorean number/music system, some of the fantasies sound similar, as does the modern emphasis upon the social construction of perception, within the sociology of knowledge, gender studies, and literary critical theory.

The element of vibrations, in all the complex variations of wave lengths, quanta, and the like, also informs the emphasis upon sophisticated communication that is regularly featured in fantastic literature. *Dreams*, for instance, which often play a large role in SF, either as the means by which beings intercommunicate, or as that activity by which they are educated, or by which their activities are modulated and controlled via psychosomatic feedback (hence dreamwork is important in futuristic projections in psychology and medicine). Again a curious resemblance to the past: the ancient healing establishment of Asklepios, the Greek god of medicine, carefully incubated dreams in which a patient was to imagine being aided and healed. And the interpretation of dream images was sufficiently developed and regularized, so that dreams might be regarded as messages from specific deities, bearing information that one would be ill-advised to ignore (White 1975; Hillman 1979).

Much SF literature asks us to imagine more eutropic/utopian realizations and developments of human potentials than we normally experience today, and likewise it points to the restricted relativity of our own historically limited consciousness. Stories of healing by means of empathic contact (the healer sending psychic feelers into the patient's body, marshaling its own inner disease-fighting mechanisms) raise questions about the poorly understood phenomenon of *spiritual healing* within our own societies. What if we were to identify and train those who already, while still youths, demonstrate marked abilities to sense somatic and psychic illness, or even to facilitate their healing? Our quickness in labeling such abilities "hogwash" may cloak our own feelings of inadequacy with respect to more appropriate relations of mind and body—certainly we never hesitate to train youths who demonstrate a special ability to play football or to merchandize soap or hamburgers or schlock magazines!

How many other human powers and capabilities do we ignore, simply because an institution such as allopathic medicine has made such giant strides? Not the least of what is good about the "new consciousness" of recent decades, for all its slick cooptation in *Mother Jones* (1976–), *Shaman's Drum* (1985–), and *New Age Quarterly* (1974–) is that the traditionally occult disciplines are explored and practiced once again—and so we hear of shamanic soul-travel, geomancy, archaeological dowsing, homeopathic healing, and so forth. Dan Noel (1997) criticizes the West's reading of shamanism and the recent development of New Age neoshamanism, while locating a more serious, respectable shamanic path in post-Jungian psychotherapy.

We are reminded of the possibilities that human consciousness is but a small part of a spectrum of consciousness that spans other animate life forms, as well as the fundamental earth powers themselves. Geomancy (*feng shui*) becomes something more than an ancient Chinese oddity when the siting of one's new home is determined by the laylines of chthonic powers earlier recognized by Native Americans in planning tribal meeting grounds, or when one builds in such a way as to take advantage of supplies of negative ions in a stream—Frank Lloyd Wright's "Fallingwater" (Waggoner 1996) must be very important to many people because it so deeply engages archetypal experience.[6]

Once again humankind is displaced from the center of the universe, as the statistical range of possibilities of various other forms and modes of advanced life among the countless galaxies begins to be recognized. Perhaps "human" does not equal "most highly evolved"; or at least SF would have us reconsider the resolutely chauvinistic pride involved in that claim (as in Piers Anthony's *Mute* (1981), where the future of civilization is assured only when humans negotiate with various psychically mutated chickens, cockroaches, and bees).

Our resolute Western egocentricity gets smashed repeatedly in SF projections of alternative social models. Sexual mores, learning patterns, communication models, social interaction networks, media of financial exchange: these and many other patterns structuring our perceived world are brought into question precisely by the creation of such different imaginings. We cannot but reflect back upon our own societies with many doubts and with a real challenge to our self-confidence; repeatedly, I have seen students engaged and challenged by surfictional probes such as Ursula Le Guin's "The Ones Who Walk Away from Omelas" (1974), whereas traditional texts on ethical issues often leave them cold.

The future-possible may exert an implicit critique of our actual past and present. Sometimes its versions do not project ahead adequately, or they cheapen the past—readers apparently love to see their own technology mapped onto more ancient societies, and so fantasy's underground caverns are lit with "strangely suspended globes of white fire," and the like. Or a primeval horde is conceived of as being no less well organized than a Wall Street brokerage firm. How often, one wonders, must the past be remade to resemble the present before we can accept its otherness? For in most slick commercial remakings (Disneyland's, Knott's Berry Farm) its otherness simply disappears as the sanitation patrols remove the daily detritus and restock the designer water dispensers (see W.G. Doty 1988).

Beginnings remain difficult to imagine; confronting us are not only countless origin/emergence/creation myths from many cultures, but attempts by contemporary authors to imagine how things were before they were so extensively technologized (William Golding's *The Inheritors* [1962] was one of the most successful, although Jean Auel's slick romances probably sold more copies). Fascination with origins, with etiological explanations, often characterizes a mythological canon. Perhaps, in a time when shared beliefs in traditional cosmogonies are rare, fantastic reconstructions are the most viable participant medium for understanding how the effective stories of our beginnings used to function: to understand the appeal of the "primitive" creation myth, we need to appreciate today's *Star Wars* trilogy and the ongoing *Star Trek: The Next Generation*.

Imaginal education must focus upon the quality of the various primal myths, must teach us to recognize how some of them—such as the Bereshith/Genesis version of human/male dominance over nature—are dangerously restrictive and short-sighted with respect to possible futures. *Imaginal education*, by teaching comparative analysis and evaluation, might instruct us in ways of finding the models of the self that will permit more comprehensive and equitable modes of interaction than those presently effective in our social structures.

We certainly need opportunities to move beyond the purely personal autobiography or biostory to the cultural mythostories that both place the individual self within a meaningful social framework and emphasize the responsibilities we carry towards one another— the corporate social responsibilities that have vanished from the careers of heroes and heroines in much of our pop culture, yet are seldom lacking in utopian fictions (see Gearhart's *Wanderground* [1978]). Given that traditional models relating the individual to communal connections have become awkward and mostly unstable, our imaginative literature (including pop culture stories) is mythologizing alternatives precisely in its future projections, and we do well to heed these projections, not uncritically, but giving them full evaluative seriousness and criticism. Transitions between the cultural models and personal selfhood may be by ways other than expensive personal psychoanalysis, if we once again respect the importance of sharing story and dream and fantasy, if we learn to devote as much attention to the hermeneutical shepherding of healthy meanings as we now do to the arithmetic calculation of tons of ballistic missiles.

Ecological optimism

We certainly have to look long and hard at our mismanagement of natural resources on this planet. Consciousness of our failures in this respect appears repeatedly in SF and fantasy, both *positively*, in terms of other (imagined) planets where there is a much more integrated balance between humans and substrate (the simple "earth" is inappropriate in terms of the wider referents here); and *negatively*, in terms of the frequent references to the death of "Old Terra," due to disasters caused by rampant radioactivity or sustained and deliberate overutilization. Eco-consciousness in this sense long predates the politics of recent ecology movements. For several generations, regional if not indeed global overpopulation has been a recurrent threat, and most elaborated SF systems project some more reasonable methods of population control than we Terrans have yet been able to devise or enforce in real time.

Or new locations for residence and employment are envisioned: undersea, underground—areas to which we have hardly begun to relate, preferring to sprawl our identical tiny single family dwellings over more and more of the landscape. Confronting the horrible jumble of competing fast food enterprises jammed together at Interstate junctions in my town, I need only review the spidery architectural site drawings of Paolo Soleri (1969) to be reminded of how seldom we give primary political attention to planning for more adequately humane urbanscapes. Astrodomes may be good enough for circuses and sports, but there is a strange dividing line between too much and too little intimacy, and surveys demonstrate that over fifty percent of Americans would prefer to live in a small town of under 10,000 people—forgetting, presumably, how cramped and limited such communities are, how lacking in the cultural resources of megalopolis.

Sadly enough, creative and sustained revisionings of *oikokosmoi* (dwelling worlds) more adequate to the actualities of our projected population size remain science fiction rather than financially and governmentally supported science reality. Many SF works sensitively explore different social topographies, and ought to receive more careful attention. They might be treated as projective mythologizations available to help us imagine improvements salvific to the crabbed and restrictive republicanism that chants only "more money to the already privileged," rather than to visions such as the European Union that takes seriously continental-wide needs for large-scale social planning, and funding.

The imaginings found in older apocalyptic projections indicate that a concern for the future eventuation of all things is one of the true characteristics of eschatological thought. Eschatology, the theory regarding how everything will eventuate, may be either utopian or dystopian, but it always claims that there are purpose and direction to history. *Future projections in SF may well be our modern eschatology.* Certainly ours is a time of widespread interest in eschatological visions, ranging from the repetitiously religious and unreal to Alvin Toffler's books, or to Robert L. Heilbroner's *An Inquiry into the Human Prospect* (1974 [1980]), or Thomas Pynchon (1975) and J.G. Ballard's (1973) complexly imbricated novels.[7] The "Apocalypse Culture" issue 4 of *21°C: Scanning the Future: A Magazine of Culture, Technology, and Science* (1995), is primarily interested in *endings* and catastrophes, but nearly every issue of this slickly produced journal has articles extrapolating *future* possibles.

The dreams of "new heavens and a new earth" in the Apocalypse to John begin to make sense as first-century SF: they become part of the imaginative spectrum that "fictionalizes" the ways we may be headed. Their symbolic elaborations remain foreign only when we have not heeded the more recent fantasy sketches that flesh out future projections in similarly non-historical ways (the feature art for *21°C* 4 transmogrifies the Four Horsemen into fantastic metallic cybertechs with detachable heads; but their laser scythes are chillingly menacing).

Is it possible to develop new visions that do not slip into the gnostic dehistoricizing? Can future projections fully reconnect mind and body in the sort of holism that refuses to pander to apocalyptic segmentation and separation of the somatic and the spiritual? I see SF and fantasy as being an important source of reflection upon this age-old problem. Facing the ecological and spiritual entropy of the end of one millennium, we can only turn desperately to "truths" whose (non-foundational) status makes us assume responsibilities earlier ascribed only to transcendental deities. We are learning, though, that "Mother Earth" may not only be a site of nurturance, but yet another raped body, whose sustenance may be nearly depleted, and is not automatically self-replenishing (Gottlieb 1996 provides a massive reader that charts the many sides of ecotheology, ecofeminism, and deep ecology).

One final aspect of SF and fantasy is optimistic where many of its other aspects are pessimistic: The emphasis upon vast stretches of time—spans of centuries, even millennia are explored—seems to reflect a basic self-confidence in human spirit, even an essential trust in the human prospect, in human history, in the utopian development of moral choices. The fictional evil agent or nasty overlord is almost always overcome in the dénouement of the plot. And perhaps the emphasis upon enormously extended reaches of time indicates a fundamental trust that humankind—or some form of higher consciousness—will win out, will endure. It seems to reflect the belief that in spite of all the desperation evoked by our racial, sexual, educational, monetary, and even nuclear catastrophes, there is likely to be some sort of noble future, albeit in previously unanticipated shapings of reality, society, existence; and only if we can remain flexible towards presently unanticipated change.

Tensing our eschatological visions by the awareness of our historical pasts; refusing those fantasies that merely recapitulate dominance models of a male-dominant, capitalist market economy; searching the range of fictional projections through the literary spectrum ranging from the formally correct to the pulp racks at the drug store: my own innate pessimism begins to ameliorate as I accept the fantastic notion that, whereas we may be here on this planet by cosmic accident, our continuance depends upon giving our attention to the range of future possibles as a matter of widespread ethical concern, as part of a more inclusive model of education that encompasses the fictional, the imaginal, and the spiritual as fully as it now emphasizes the hard mechanical sciences of the body and matter.[8]

Libby/Andy suggests to Lazarus, in Heinlein's classic, *Methusalah's Children* (1941 [1967]) that "Maybe there aren't any reasons." Lazarus bows off the last page of this massive future history:

> "Yes, maybe it is just one colossal big joke, with no point to it." Lazarus stood up and stretched and scratched his ribs. "But I can tell you, Andy, whatever the answers are, here's one monkey that's going to keep on climbing, and looking around him to see what he can see, as long as the tree holds out."
>
> (830)

Appendix I: Fiction

At the suggestion of one of the editors, I have included sample references for each writer mentioned; since reprint versions often obtain, here with exceptions, I give date of the initial publication only:

Anthony, Piers (1981) *Mute*, Seven Oaks: New English Library.
Auel, Jean (1980) *The Clan of the Cave Bear*, New York: Crown.
Ballard, J.G. (1973) *Crash*, New York: Vintage.
Bear, Gregory (1990) *Queen of Angels*, New York: Warner Books.
Gearhart, Sally Miller (1978) *The Wanderground: Stories of the Hill Women*, Watertown, MA: Persephone Press.
Gibson, William (1984) *Neuromancer*, London: HarperCollins.
Golding, William (1954) *Lord of the Flies*, London: Faber & Faber.
—— (1962) *The Inheritors*, London: Faber & Faber.
Healy, Raymond J. and Francis McComas, J. (eds) (1946) *Adventures in Time and Space: An Anthology of Science Fiction Stories*, New York: Ballantine; 2nd edn, 1975.
Heinlein, Robert A. (1967) *The Past Through Tomorrow* (the Future History Stories, 1939–58 in 1 vol.), London: New English Library.
Herbert, Frank (1965–) *Dune* (the series), New York: Putnam.
Le Guin, Ursula (1969) *The Left Hand of Darkness*, New York: Ace Books.
—— (1974) "The Ones Who Walk Away from Omelas," in Terry Carr (ed.) *The Best Science Fiction of the Year: 3*, New York: Ballantine, 273–80.
—— (1996) "Mountain Ways," *Asimov's Science Fiction* 20/8, 14–39.
Orwell, George (1949) *1984*, London; Secker & Warburg.
Pynchon, Thomas (1975) *Gravity's Rainbow*, New York: Penguin.
Wolfe, Tom (1979) *The Right Stuff*, New York: Farrar, Strauss & Giroux.

Appendix II: Ilustrations

1 *The Ophite Diagram*: The earthly cosmos consists of body, soul, and spirit. In the middle is the earth with the underworld (*Tartaros*). Around it in concentric circles are the sphere of Behemoth/ Atmosphere; the spheres of the seven planets/Leviathan; the circle of the fixed stars, in which the signs of the zodiac and paradise appear. Adapted from Rudolph (1983: 68–9), citing the German version (1955: 32).

2 Signs (characters) and Seals of the aeons, according to the Coptic books of Jeu 174; from Schmidt (1962: 278–369).

Notes

1   Citation can be found in James Traub's book notice in the *New York Times Book Review* section (19 April 1981: 12).

2   Gnosticism was an intellectual and spiritual movement that was coalescing just before the first century of the Common Era, as a culmination of Hellenistic syncretistic fantasies that peaked a century or so later. It combined elements of Greek, Roman, and Ancient Near-Eastern mysticism and ideologies with Jewish and Christian ideas and mythologems, then phased into various types of hermeticism and underground mysticism. Jonas (1963) remains the best introduction to the aspects of gnosticism mentioned in this essay. Robinson (1977) makes available standardized translations for the gnostic Christian texts found in Egypt in 1945. Pagels (1979) provides a useful political contextualization of the process by which orthodox Christianity excluded the quite considerable gnostic portions of earliest Christianity.

3   See Wolfe's (1979) account of the indignities visited upon the initial group of US astronauts. Thompson (1981: 34–5) cleverly reads Nicholas Roeg's film *The Man Who Fell to Earth* as a gnostic fantasy. Dutton's (1995) amply illustrated volume sharply interrogates Western ideals of masculine beauty, and problematizes the ways Christianity has both idealized the body (incarnation) and despised it (asceticism).

4   The title of Noel's *Approaching Earth: A Search for the Mythic Significance of the Space Age* (1986) reflects some of the ideological issues involved in our necessary re-sighting of ourselves after our initial, but epochal exploits in space. Lippard (1983, 1990) and Gablik (1995) document richly how contemporary artists have come to new appreciations of our planet, in a postmodern period of rediscovering ourselves from the vantage points of other times and peoples.

5   Certainly *Zeitgeist*, ideology, and mythical models shape historical movements. Gearhart (1991) demonstrates how a putative "myth of matriarchy" was influential in the women's movements of the mid 1960s; Girling (1993) documents instances in the USA, Germany, and UK.

6   "Geomancy . . . is a means of unifying, at a specific moment, the psyche with natural circumstances. It is a mechanism of insight which permits a fantasy of meaning to be imposed upon a situation" (O'Connor 1980: 58).

7   Eddins (1984, 1990) convincingly demonstrate gnostic and Kabbalistic elements of Pynchon's apocalyptic.

8   After writing the initial draft of this essay, I came upon Hassan (1975: chap. 6), "The New Gnosticism: Speculations on an Aspect of the Postmodern Mind." That essay expands the analytic developed here to include technology and non-SF literature; we seem mostly in agreement on the major issues, but work on quite different materials. I am grateful to Patrick E. Green and Elizabeth A. Meese for the sorts of encouraging scourings of one's writing that keep writers writing.

8

RETROFITTING GNOSTICISM

Philip K. Dick and Christian origins

Michel Desjardins

Philip K. Dick (1928–82), a major twentieth-century US literary figure who published forty-two novels and more than 115 short stories, has attracted considerable scholarly attention (e.g. Barlow 1988; Butler 1995; Olander and Greenberg 1983; Sutin 1989, 1995; Warrick 1987; Williams 1986. His work contributed to four movies (*Blade Runner, Total Recall, Screamers, Confessions d'un Barjo*) and an opera (*VALIS*).[1] It continues to inspire a loyal following (Sutin 1989: xi–xiv), particularly in science fiction circles.

Gnosticism entered Dick's life in 1974 during a series of visionary experiences which he subsequently came to understand as essentially "gnostic"—not the popular New Age/Jungian mix which now often passes for gnosticism (see Hoeller 1982; Segal 1992; Singer 1992), but the second-century mode of Christian expression considered heretical by the early Church Fathers, and reflected more positively in the ancient writings discovered in 1945 near the Egyptian town of Nag Hammadi. During the last eight years of his life, Dick read many of the Nag Hammadi texts, familiarized himself with the leading secondary studies in the academic study of gnosticism, and integrated these ideas into his public and private writings. He was *au courant* with gnosticism before it became common outside academic circles, and to a degree rarely seen among non-specialists.

This essay explores the gnostic elements in Dick's work and reflects on their implications. It posits significant points of contact between his *œuvre* and themes found in second- and third-century Christian texts usually considered gnostic, supporting his appropriation of this religious paradigm. Much has changed in the field of gnostic studies since Dick's day. From the late 1950s to the early 1980s, Hans Jonas' (1963) work dominated the North American view of gnosticism. Dick derived much from Jonas' *The Gnostic Religion: The Message of the Alien God and the Beginnings of Christianity*, which is philosophical (Heidegger; existentialism) and holistic (assuming a single "gnostic spirit" in antiquity) in nature. Fueled by emerging analyses of the Nag Hammadi texts, the last two decades have witnessed, first, a heightened appreciation of the social settings lying behind texts long considered gnostic, and second, rising skepticism about the coherence of such a religio-philosophical movement. Nevertheless, "gnosticism" perdures in scholarly circles; it is the revised, modern paradigm exemplified by Kurt Rudolph's *Gnosis: The Nature and History of Gnosticism* (1983), which I am applying here to Dick's work.

Blade Runner offers a challenging point of entry to this discussion. Adapted from Dick's 1968 novel, *Do Androids Dream of Electric Sheep?*, Ridley Scott's movie was released three months after Dick's death in 1982; *Blade Runner: The Director's Cut*, which appeared in 1992, became considerably more popular than the initial theatrical release.[2] During the preparation of this movie, Dick had several much publicized disagreements with the screen adaptation of his novel, and for good reasons: the movie introduces significant changes to the novel, ignoring many of the nuances in tone (e.g. Dick's usual humor and irony) and context (e.g. Deckard's marriage; the extermination of animals on earth) (see Fitting 1987; Sutin 1989; Sammon 1996). Close ties, however, remain between the book and the movie.

The story line is both simple and ambiguous. In a dark and rainy, post-apocalyptic Los Angeles in the year 2019, a small group of "Nexus 6" androids ("replicants," as Scott preferred to call them) has broken the law by returning to earth from an "offworld" site. Deckard (Harrison Ford), a former bounty hunter previously involved in the extermination of replicants, is coerced into taking on his former duties. The narrative follows him as he successfully participates in the death of each of these replicants. Character representations complicate matters. Deckard, for instance, is likely a replicant himself, although he may not realize it until the final scene, if at all. As the story unfolds, he falls in love with Rachael (Sean Young), herself a new form of replicant who works for Tyrell (Joe Turkel), the creator of all the replicants; the closing scene has Deckard and Rachael escaping together in the hope that she can avoid extermination. In addition, the replicants (Rutger Hauer, the leader, as Roy Batty; Joanna Cassidy as Zhora; Daryl Hannah as Pris; Brion James as Leon) are portrayed with considerable sympathy. Programmed to live for only four years, they have come to earth to seek extended life from their creator. The movie climaxes with Roy's dying words: "I've seen things you people wouldn't believe. . . . All those moments will be lost in time, like tears in rain. Time to die."

A gnostic filter offers a coherent view of *Blade Runner*. First, clues abound that Tyrell represents a Demiurge figure. Like the gnostic "Yahweh," he too is an inferior deity (the biblically maligned "God [*El*] of Tyre"), rules his domain, creates beings who not only resemble but surpass him, acts the role of father (in one version of the movie, one of Roy's last phrases to his creator is, "I want more life, Father"),[3] and is linked to ecclesiastical power (Tyrell's bedroom is decorated in papal style; like the Pope, he wears a large ring on his little finger).

Second, one can substitute the movie's replicants for gnosticism's humans. The gnostic scenario is one in which humans are created by the Demiurge to serve him, are given a terminal life span, yet contain an essence which makes them greater than their creator. In the movie, the replicants are created "more human than human" by Tyrell, with a four-year life span, and their role is to serve humans ("Nexus" also brings to mind "binding").

Third, the dominant gnostic symbol of light to represent spirituality is reinforced by the near total absence of natural light in this *film noir*. With the exception of one brief rooftop scene, artificial light is the only form of illumination in the never-ending smoke and rain. Darkness in this movie is complemented by the importance placed on eyes: the movie opens with an eye that fills the screen, another scene occurs in a genetic laboratory which makes replicant eyes, replicants often murder by gouging someone's eyes, Pris' makeup accentuates her eyes, Roy jests with the genetic designer Sebastian (William Sanderson) by using bulging eyes, and Tyrell hides his eyes behind enormous glasses.

Fourth, the Christ figure so often highlighted in extant gnostic texts finds a partial parallel with Roy. His name allows for this possibility ("Roy" as "king"; more hypothetically, "Batty" as "bythos/abyss," a term often connected to the gnostic spiritual principle). Roy's dying words ("I've seen things you people wouldn't believe") transfix Deckard; more Christologically-charged still are the closing scenes, where he sticks a nail through his hand, then releases a white dove as he dies.

Fifth, gnosticism's persistent search for origins (From where do we come? To where are we going?) accords with the importance the movie places on memories. Tyrell implants false memories with corresponding photographs in his replicants; they treasure their collection of photographs as they ponder their roots, which are in fact different from those they imagine.

Sixth, just as the gnostic texts focus on awakening humans (often the "psychics") to the spiritual realm, so too do we observe Deckard's sluggish path to self-knowledge. He tests others to see whether they are replicants, but has not tested himself. Yet he too has his photographs. His moment of revelation appears to come at the end when he picks up an origami figure of a unicorn, one of several deposited throughout the movie by a colleague, Gaff (Edward James Olmos). The figure accords with one of Deckard's previous dreams ("Director's Cut" version), available to Gaff only if Deckard's dreams and memories are common knowledge.

The seventh and last link concerns gender. Mirroring the importance placed on female figures by early gnostics, the movie highlights three female replicants. Their names suggest deeper meaning, although specific connections are difficult to pinpoint—for instance, "Zhora" in Greek means "pure/undefiled;" "Pris" brings to mind Homer's "Aphrodite Kypris"; and "Rachael" has roots in the semitic divine *El*. Yet despite the importance of a female divine principle in some gnostic texts, academics (e.g. King 1988) now increasingly recognize a persistent devaluation of the female in the sources. This movie offers the same mix. Pris and Zhora are created as sex objects; Rachael, at first looking like an animated barbie doll, is treated crudely by Deckard and the cityscape images of female Asian figures reinforce the image of the female as alien/lesser than the male. The extraordinarily brutal killings of both Zhora and Pris, coupled with the suggestion of Rachael's underlying purity, suggest that *Blade Runner*'s ambivalent presentation of its female characters points to more than the ever-present sexism reflected in popular movies. Like early Christian forms of gnosticism, this movie significantly elevates and denigrates "the female."

This gnostic assessment of *Blade Runner* is more fully grounded in Dick's life and writings. Two visionary experiences led him directly to gnosticism.[4] The first occurred in 1963 when he saw an enormous, slotted-eyed face staring down at him from the sky. He would later call this figure the "God of Wrath";[5] still later, he would equate it with the gnostic Demiurge.[6] The second, more important, vision came a decade later, in the winter of 1974, following a troubled period in his life, which included a recent separation from his fourth wife, and a suicide attempt. One day as he opened the door to his house, a fish pendant on a delivery person's neck caught his attention.

When the wearer described it as an early Christian symbol, Dick, as he tells us (see Platt 1980: 145–8), felt a force flow through him: a pink light that would revisit him several times over the next few weeks to impart what felt like a staggering amount of information. Enough of it was patently revelatory (e.g. diagnosing his son's previously unknown life-threatening ailment) to give him reason to consider seriously the visionary elements which at first made no sense to him.

And ponder he did. From 1974 to his death eight years later he kept a hand-written journal, his "Exegesis," in which he reflected on this episode. It would come to contain over two million words.[7] The journal and his later publications reveal a growing interest in God;[8] they show that his explorations led him to various esoteric traditions, including the Dead Sea Scrolls (Dick 1982) and the Kabbalah (Dick 1981a). But it was his discovery of the Nag Hammadi Library in the late 1970s that made him think that the revelatory light had been nothing else but ancient gnosticism *redivivus*. Consequently, Dick read voraciously in the field. By 1980 he had become, in his words, "something of an authority" on gnosticism (Butler 1995: 228). With this grounding in gnosticism came the conviction that he had been chosen to reveal anew the wisdom that the world as we know it is but an imperfect, illusory expression of a more fundamental reality, and that a new savior was about to appear to make this reality fully manifest.

He recounts this journey from vision to insight in his lightly fictionalized novel, *VALIS* (completed in 1978 [1981b]).[9] The book presents two narrative personae of the author himself: "Phil" and "Horselover Fat" (an etymological play on the Greek word for "Philip" and the German one for "Dick"), who struggle to come to terms with Dick's own unsettling visionary experience of 1974. Phil the rationalist, insisting that Fat's visionary knowledge, authentic or not, makes no sense, is set off against Fat the mystic, who knows the truth of what he experienced. Theological arguments fill the first nine chapters, as the characters—including Kevin the nihilist and David the Catholic—attempt to address Fat's experience and determine how one verifies a genuine theophany. Gnosticism stands front and center in this discussion, particularly after Fat's psychiatrist introduces him to the Nag Hammadi Library. "Basically," Fat declares, "my doctrine is Valentinian, second century CE" (1981b: 86). *VALIS*'s last six chapters witness the group setting off in search of the incarnated savior. They succeed in finding her (Sophia) and resolve their differences, but after her accidental death their uncertainties and differences re-emerge and remain unresolved. The book ends with Fat traveling the world in search of another savior.

By the late 1970s, Dick began to notice that his earlier writings also were gnostic.[10] His journal explores the paradox of how he could have presented a gnostic viewpoint during a time when he knew nothing about gnosticism, of how the post-1974 ideas find their way into his pre-1974 fantasy writings—and, one might now add, how they find their way into a film adaptation of a 1968 novel. What explains the radical gnostic critique of the cosmos underlying his countercultural stance? Dick found a partial answer in his reflections on the nature of time. He came to believe that time is not divisible into the simple categories of "past," "present" and "future." Occasionally, it can literally stand still;[11] sometimes actions can be repeated and anticipated. He became particularly intrigued by situations described in his books which later came to life for him exactly as he had narrated them (Dick 1986; reprinted in Sutin 1995: 259–80). These musings concerning time allowed Dick to give additional credence to his pre-visionary "gnostic" ideas.

Historians of religion will note a striking parallel between Philip Dick and Carl Jung. Jung likewise developed his idea of archetypes before discovering them anew in gnostic texts. Later in life he would say that the ancient gnostics already knew what it took him years to discover. The parallel does not stop there. Jung also claimed to have had a gnostic vision. In 1916, as he recounts it, he felt a spirit enter his house and infuse him with radically new thoughts. Out of this experience came *The Seven Sermons to the Dead*, a book he did not publicly reveal until later in his career (see Hoeller 1982; Segal 1992). There is another point of similarity: Jung's vision, like Dick's, came at a time of crisis, just after he had severed his strong ties with Freud. For both Jung and Dick, then, a later awareness of gnosticism grew out of intense personal experiences, and helped to put their entire work in sharper focus.

Dick's assessment of the gnostic flavor of his own writings, both before and after his visionary experience in 1974, has considerable textual support—more than he himself recognized, I would argue, if one situates his work in the context of gnostic studies in the 1990s.[12] Of particular note are the following five, interrelated points which were important, *inter alia*, to both Dick and the ancient gnostics.

First and foundational, Dick's work shows strong opposition to forms of constraint and confinement. His stories often present situations in which people struggle to free themselves from the clutches of someone or something more powerful. In *The Divine Invasion* (1981a), for instance, the world is seen to be a creation of the fictional equivalent of the Demiurge. This stance is also reflected in the "castrating bitches" model for many of his female characters (e.g. Fay in *Confessions of a Crap Artist* [1975]) which develops out of his own life experiences, and reveals a blatant misogynistic strain to much of his work.[13] At times the struggle tumbles into paranoia. Dick's characters often suspect that not only everyone but everything is out to get them. This rebellious mood—that we live in a world dominated by strong forces which we need to recognize and resist—is quintessentially gnostic (the paranoia is not). Indeed, the "cosmic anti-Semitism" so often found in the gnostic texts might well parallel the anger against women displayed in Dick's work: anger directed at the God of the Bible and at women both reflect attempts to break free from a dominant matrix.

A second issue builds on the first: the world is not as we know it; neither is humanity's place in it. Dick's projection of human problems and solutions onto other worlds and times emerges from the disharmony he felt with his own world. Like the characters in *The Man in the High Castle*, in his view, we inhabit a world in which "madmen are in power" (see Malmgren 1980: 120–30). Dick deliberately cultivated a chaotic writing style in order to reflect what he perceived as an unwelcoming reality. The "Exegesis" too reveals Dick's particular fascination with disharmony.[14] Gnostic writers for whom the once stable Judeo-Christian world of a good God and a comforting creation has been overturned often display a similar perspective, and at times a similar writing style. According to these writers, gnosis reveals the essential unreality of the present world; it identifies the spiritual domain as the locus of harmony and stability.

A third issue also complements the first: unequivocal, absolute paradigms oppress; reality needs to be explored using a variety of myths and with a spirit of openness. Dick was rarely pleased with clear-cut representations. His own sense of alienation from the world did not lead him to posit simple alternatives, and his answers to questions of good and evil, truth and error, remained flexible and occasionally indeterminate. A good example of the latter is his depiction of Fat (one of his own personae) by Phil (another persona) in *VALIS*:

> It strikes me as an interesting paradox that a Buddha—an enlightened one—would be unable to figure out, even after four-and-a-half years, that he had become enlightened. Fat had become totally bogged down in his enormous exegesis,

trying futilely to determine what had happened to him. He resembled more a hit-and-run accident victim than a Buddha.

(1981b: 122)

Even a direct encounter with the revelatory light is not enough to convince Fat; the same can be said for Herb Asher (*The Divine Invasion* [1981a]) after his personal encounter with God, and Bishop Archer (*The Transmigration of Timothy Archer* [1982]) after he communicates with his dead son. Revelation extends beyond the rational; one can only approach it obliquely. Christian gnostics seem to have shared this viewpoint. Church Fathers (see Rudolph 1983: 53) complained about what they perceived as the frightening array of gnostic theories and speculations. More recently, some Nag Hammadi texts have suggested that ambivalence and uncertainty formed a surprisingly important part of gnostic thinking. Gnostics may have preached enlightenment by enlightened ones, but their *gnosis* nevertheless did not turn practitioners into Buddhas: their stories constantly shifted, they remained fearful of death (e.g. the closing of *The Second Apocalypse of James*, in Robinson 1988), they designed a series of rituals in order to lead them along the spiritual path one step at a time, and they seemed as concerned with improper thoughts and actions as were their Jewish and Christian co-religionists (Desjardins 1990). Enlightenment did not end the questing.

A fourth issue is epistemological in nature: meaning, or salvation, comes from within, and often needs to be sparked by an outside revealer. Dick emphasized people's connections with others, rather than to the state or religious institution, as a means to awaken one's true self. He saw "reality" grounded in individuals. "You will have no other gods but yourselves" is the refrain from *VALIS*, a point reinforced in his earlier novel, *The Cosmic Puppets* (1957), which presents the deities "Ohrmazd" and "Ahirman" fighting each other, with little care for humans. Gnostic texts affirm the same principle: the "kingdom is within" (e.g. *The Gospel of Thomas* 3; 51, in Robinson 1988), and saviors remind people of the redemptive force that lies within them. In Christian gnostic circles, Jesus' death is not so much what "saves." Rather, it is his message of the individual's own power of liberation.

The relationship of the created with the creator is the fifth issue. Throughout his career Dick kept returning to the issue of androids becoming greater than their creators. Androids play a part in no less than six of his novels and ten of his short stories, a fascination which at first derived from Dick's conviction that they were both alien and dangerous (see his first android story, "Second Variety" [1953]; turned into the movie *Screamers* [1996]), and which later developed to seeing more human-like qualities to them. A fundamental gnostic belief is that humans, although created by a divine figure, once enlightened will recognize that they are essentially superior to their creator. A "phildickian" might call the gnostic texts "android literature."

These five points of overlap between Dick and the early gnostics take us further than a California science fiction writer and his fascination with gnosticism. Dick's gnostic concerns place him in the company of the Cathars (twelfth- and thirteenth-century France), Manichaeans (third-century Syria through seventeenth-century China), and Mandaeans (Iraq from pre-Christian times to the present), to name just a few of the well-known gnostic groups with clear parallels to the gnostics of the ancient Mediterranean world.[15] To probe beneath the surface of Dick's writings in this instance is to discover a persistent gnostic stratum.

Dick's gnostic worldview is also grounded more broadly in his own life context. To come to this realization is to return to one of Clifford Geertz's insights, applicable to literary analysis as well as ethnography, that any interpreter is faced with "a multiplicity of complex conceptual structures, many of them superimposed upon or knotted into one another, which are at once strange, irregular and inexplicit" and need to be explored "by going beneath the surface" (1973: 10). Geertz calls this process of digging deeper "thick description." Ever fascinated by coincidences and synchronicity, Dick would have enjoyed the idea of a "thick" description of "Fat"—one that moved the interpretation from "science fiction" to "gnostic experience" to "human experience."

A "thick description" of Dick includes links to his social context. Much of his life was spent in California, and many of his publications are situated, as Carl Freedman (1988) reminds us, between the Kennedy assassination in 1963 and the Watergate scandal and the end of the Vietnam War in the early 1970s. For many Americans, this was a time of conspiracies, deceptions, and a countercultural fear of "the system." Is it any wonder that Dick wrote about such matters? Or that one of his most enduring interpreters and supporters has been Paul Williams (1986), formerly a writer for *Rolling Stone*? One might add that Dick's increasing use of amphetamines and alcohol, and his exposure to hard drugs (particularly in the early 1970s), would naturally have accentuated his sense of alienation from the world around him.

Regardless of their specific origins, the themes that emerge in both Dick and the gnostics tap into more universal longings: humans are significant and individuals can make a difference; we are now oppressed by large and powerful forces which alienate us from our potential; other realities exist; and the present situation can change for the better. How are these themes expressed? We hear stories about Yahweh and Tyrell, heaven and other "offworld" sites, angels and androids, beings who oppress and others who are oppressed. The stories express alienation combined with longing for justice and truth. This is gnosticism. It is also Philip Dick. To be sure, it is far more than this—extending deeply, for instance, into modern culture. I think of *X-Files*, with its mottoes: "Trust no one" and "The truth is out there." In this popular television series (created and produced by Chris Carter), Dana Scully (played by Gillian Anderson) and Fox Mulder (David Duchovny), mid 1990s variants of *VALIS*'s "Phil" and "Fat," offer alternate reactions to the possibility of extranormal existence: Scully is the scientific skeptic while Mulder is ever ready to accept para-rational solutions and realities. Mulder and Fat (with their shadow partners both distinguishing and completing them) are able to see possibilities which lie beyond our normal world, providing counter realities for some today just as the gnostics did in their day.

These modern heroes are biblically grounded, as were the gnostics of old. In fact, their narratives often emerge from "misreadings" of biblical stories (Bloom 1975). Biblical paradigms and myths endure, but often in altered forms, be it the gnostic demotion of God, or the female savior in Dick's *VALIS*. Readers continue to seek meaning in biblical stories, and interpret them subversively (e.g. feminist, liberationist readings) in order to counter dominant ideologies. But for many today the Bible also represents the "establishment" (Christian and Jewish) position they find limiting (Will anything change if the Bible continues to be seen as sacred? How can we progress using texts which are two to three thousand years old?). New fantasy is needed, as Rosemary Jackson reminds us, to address "an order experienced as oppressive and insufficient" (1988: 180).

Dick's stories, intertwined with esoteric traditions, set on other worlds and in other times, offer a new form of an old paradigm. Like early Christians, gnostic or otherwise, he was dissatisfied with his world, worked diligently to make others equally dissatisfied, and through his stories offered positive alternatives and hope for transformation. More self-consciously than early Christians, he expressed those stories through the medium of fantasy. Still, their points of overlap remain striking, and Dick's explorations remain one of the few modern instances in which retrofitting gnosticism has kept the form of the original.

Notes

1 *Blade Runner* is based on the novel, *Do Androids Dream of Electric Sheep?* (1968, written 1966); *Total Recall* is based on "We Can Remember it for you Wholesale" (1966, written 1965); *Screamers* is based on *Second Variety* (1953, written 1952) and *Barjo* is based on *Confessions of a Crap Artist* (1975, written 1959). The opera *VALIS*, created by Tod Machover, premièred at the Centre Georges Pompidou, Paris in 1987, and has since played throughout the world (see Machover [1987]; Bowden [1988]).

2 There were, in fact, seven versions of *Blade Runner* (see Sammon 1993); two remain in circulation: the 1982 theatrical release and the 1992 "Director's Cut."

3 Both the theatrical release and the director's cut versions have "I want more life, fucker." A "workprint" edition, first screened in England in 1982, then briefly revived in Los Angeles in 1991 (then called the "Director's Cut," but the title was dropped), has "I want more life, father" (Sammon 1993).

4 Dick had other visions after these, which he saw as complementing his earlier ones (see Sutin 1989: 269–84). In his journal, he reflected on two of them. One (17 November 1980) revealed to him a loving and kind God; in the second (17 September 1981) he saw a vision of a dark-skinned savior, the "second incarnation of Christ." For vital connections between visionary states and gnosticism, see Merkur (1993).

5 See his novel *Deus Irae* (1976), which takes up this issue directly. The context is a destroyed USA, with someone in search of Carlton Lufteufel (the devil, the "God of Wrath"), the one responsible for dropping the bomb.

6 Barlow (1988: 26) notes that the 1963 vision led Dick to seek refuge in Episcopalianism in the hope of finding a benign deity. On this topic see the comment by Nancy Hackett, one of Dick's wives: "When I met Phil at the end of 1964, he had recently become an Episcopalian. He took this very seriously. . . . He was a man beset by fears and insecurity. . . . The one Christian doctrine he clung to all the time I knew him was The Judgement. He was terrified of Judgement Day. He would spend hours contemplating this with sweat literally dripping down his face" (letter 1988).

7 Only extracts of the "Exegesis" are available (see Sutin 1991). Dick's estate has yet to release the entire work.

8 See Barlow 1988: 291–326. Dick's last speech to a science fiction audience (Metz, France, 1977; Dick 1978) focused on his experience of God. The two-hour presentation was not well received from an audience of mainly agnostic science fiction writers.

9 For an analysis of *VALIS* in the context of *The Divine Invasion* (1981a) and *The Transmigration of Timothy Archer* (1982), see Galbreath (1983). An earlier form of *VALIS*, accepted for publication in 1976 appeared as *Radio Free Albemuth* (1985).

10 Dick explored the gnostic nature of his entire work in his "Exegesis." The importance of gnosticism for Dick has also not escaped the notice of scholars (e.g. Dumont 1988; Galbreath 1982; MacKay 1984), although scholars of gnosticism have paid little attention to Dick. See also the leader article by Jay Kinney on Dick in the opening issue of *Gnosis* magazine in 1985, expanded in the introduction to Sutin's *In Pursuit of VALIS*.

11 Both his "Exegesis" and *VALIS* present a form of dispensationalism in which the progress of time ceased when the Christian gnostic texts were buried (he claims this occurred in the second century; the texts were buried in the fourth), only to start anew when they were discovered in 1945.

12 Others, to be sure, have seen the importance of religion in Dick's work. Umland, for example, states "I have come to the conclusion that Dick cannot be understood fully except by approaching him through the great historiographers and hermeneuticists of esoteric religion and the occult: Hans Jonas, Mircea Eliade, Gershom Scholem, and, above all, Carl Jung" (1995: 94).

13 The recent biography of Dick by one of his wives, Anne Dick, highlights this misogyny; according to Sutin (1989: 277), Dick himself acknowledged that before the publication of his *The Divine Invasion* (1981a) his depiction of female characters had "been inadequate and even sometimes vicious."

14 See Sutin:

> His most persistent starting point was the "two-source cosmogony" discussed in *VALIS*: our apparent but false universe (*natura naturata*, *maya*, *dokos*, Satan) is partially redeemed by its ongoing blending with the genuine source of being (*natura naturans*, *brahman*, *eidos*, God). Together the two sources—set and ground—create a sort of holographic universe that deceives us. Disentangling reality from illusion is the goal of enlightenment, and the essence of enlightenment is Plato's *anamnêsis* (as in 2–3–74 [a standardized form of his visionary experience of February–March 1994]): recalling the eternal truths known to our souls prior to our birth in this realm. But enlightenment is a matter of grace. God bestows it at the height of our extremity, in response to our need and readiness to receive the truth. These are Phil's basic themes in the *Exegesis*.
>
> (1989: 264)

15 See Richard Smith's "Afterword" (in Robinson 1988: 532–49) for an overview of writers and other artists influenced by gnosticism.

BIBLIOGRAPHY

Acker, K. (1966) "Of Death and Desire," *Culture Jam, 21°C: Scanning the Future: A Magazine of Culture, Technology, and Science*, 8, 10–11.

Adorno, Theodor (1990) "On Popular Music," in Simon Frith and Andrew Goodwin (eds) *On Record: Rock, Pop, and the Written Word*, London: Routledge, 301–14.

Aichele, George (1996) *Jesus Framed*, Biblical Limits, London: Routledge.

Allen, Woody (1972) *Without Feathers*, New York: Warner Books.

Altizer, Thomas J.J. (1985) *History As Apocalypse*, Albany, NY: State University of New York Press.

Amstutz, Wendell (1992) *Information, Insight, Help and Hope for Destructive Beliefs, Behaviors, Influences*, Columbia, MO: Charter Hospital. (Booklet distributed at Satanism and Psychiatry workshop.)

Arens, W. (1979) *The Man-Eating Myth*, New York: Oxford University Press.

Attali, Jacques (1977) *Bruits: essai sur l'économie politique de la musique*, Paris: Presses Universitaires de France; *Noise: the Political Economy of Music*, trans. Brian Massumi, foreword by Frederic Jameson, afterword by Susan McClary, Theory and History of Literature, vol. 16, Minneapolis, MN: University of Minnesota Press, 1985.

Axlbio.html (1997) Biography of Axl Rose (World Wide Web page), http://www.students.uiuc.edu/7Et-gray/axlbio.html.

Bachelard, Gaston (1964a) *The Poetics of Space*, trans. Maria Jolas, Boston, MA: Beacon.

—— (1964b) *The Psychoanalysis of Fire*, trans. Alan C.M. Ross, Boston, MA: Beacon.

Bakhtin, Mikhail Mikhailovich (1984) *Rabelais and His World*, trans. Hélène Iswolsky, foreword by Krystyna Pomorska, prologue by Michael Holquist, Bloomington, IN: Indiana University Press.

Bal, Mieke (1987) *Lethal Love: Feminist Literary Readings of Biblical Love Stories*, Bloomington, IN: Indiana University Press.

Ballard, J.G. (1973) *Crash*, New York: Vintage.

Bamberger, Bernard J. (1971) "Nephilim," *Encyclopedia Judaica*, vol. 12, Jerusalem: Keter Publishing House.

Barfield, Owen (1977) *The Rediscovery of Meaning, and Other Essays*, Middletown, CT: Wesleyan University Press.

Barker, Margaret (1992) *The Great Angel: A Study of Israel's Second God*, Louisville, KY: Westminster/John Knox.

Barlow, A.J. (1988) "Reality, Religion and Politics in Philip K. Dick's Fiction," unpublished Ph.D. dissertation, University of Iowa.

Barthes, Roland (1972) *Mythologies*, trans. Annette Lavers, New York: Hill & Wang.

Bataille, Georges (1986) *Eroticism: Death and Sensuality*, trans. Mary Dalwood, San Francisco, CA: City Lights Books.

Baudrillard, Jean (1990) *Seduction*, trans. Brian Singer, New York: St Martin's Press.

Bauer, Walter (1957) *A Greek-English Lexicon of the New Testament and Other Early Christian Literature*, trans. William F. Arndt and F. Wilbur Gingrich, Chicago, IL: University of Chicago and Cambridge: Cambridge University Press.

Blade Runner (1982) Ridley Scott (dir.) Blade Runner Partnership/Ladd Company.

Blade Runner: The Director's Cut (1992) Ridley Scott (dir.) Blade Runner Partnership/Ladd Company.

Blake, L.D. (1990) "Comments on Genesis: Chapter V," in E.C. Stanton (ed.) *The Woman's Bible*, Seattle, WA: Coalition Task Force on Women and Religion.

Blenkinsopp, Joseph (1990) *Ezekiel*, Interpretation: A Bible Commentary for Teaching and Preaching, Louisville, KY: Westminster/John Knox.

Blish, James (1964) *The Issue At Hand*, Chicago, IL: Advent. (Collection of critical reviews written under the pseudonym William Atheling, Jr.)

—— (1982a) *Black Easter*, New York: Avon; first published, 1968.

—— (1982b) *The Day After Judgment*, New York: Avon; first published, 1971.

—— (1987) "Probapossible Prolegomena to Idereal History," in Cy Chauvin (ed.) *The Tale that Wags the God*, Chicago, IL: Advent.

—— (1990) *Devil's Day*, New York: Baen Books. (Combined publication of *Black Easter* and *The Day After Judgment*.)

—— (1991) *After Such Knowledge*, London: Arrow Books. (One volume compilation of *Doctor Mirabilis* [1964], *Black Easter* [1968], *Day After Judgment* [1971], and *A Case of Conscience* [1959]).

Bloom, H. (1975) *A Map of Misreading*, New York: Oxford University Press.

—— (1996) *Omens of Millenium: The Gnosis of Angels, Dreams, and Resurrection*, New York: Riverhead Books.

Bloom, H. and Rosenberg, D. (trans.) (1990) *The Book of J*, New York: Grove Weidenfeld.

Boer, Roland (1997) *Novel Histories: the Fiction of Biblical Criticism*, Playing the Text, Sheffield: Sheffield Academic Press.

Borges, Jorge Luis (1962) *Ficciones*, trans. and ed. Anthony Kerrigan, New York: Grove Press.

Born, Georgina (1993) "Afterword: Music Policy, Aesthetic and Social Difference," in Tony Bennett, *et al.* (eds) *Rock and Popular Music: Politics, Policies, Institutions*, Culture: Policies and Politics, London and New York: Routledge, 266–92.

Bowden, K. (1988) "VALIS—The Opera," *The Philip K. Dick Society Newsletter*, 17, 8.

Broch, Hermann (1932) *The Sleepwalkers*, trans. Willa and Edwin Muir, New York: Little, Brown; first published in German *Die Schlafwandler*, 1932.

Brown, K. Mc Carthy (1991) *Mama Lola. A Vodou Priestess in Brooklyn*, San Francisco, CA: University of California Press.

Brownlee, William H. (1986) *Ezekiel 1–19*, Word Biblical Commentary, Waco, TX: Word Books.

Brueggemann, Walter (1982) *Genesis: A Bible Commentary for Teaching and Preaching*, Atlanta, GA: John Knox Press.

Bulwer-Lytton, Edward (1871) *The Coming Race*, John Weeks (ed.) Santa Barbara, CA: Woodbridge Press, 1989.

Butler, A.M. (1995) "Ontology and Ethics in the Writings of Philip K. Dick," unpublished Ph.D. dissertation, Hull University, UK.

Buxton, David (1990) "Rock Music, the Star System, and the Rise of Consumerism," in Simon Frith and Andrew Goodwin (eds) *On Record: Rock, Pop, and the Written Word*, London: Routledge, 427–40.

Cameron, Ron (ed.) (1982) *The Other Gospels*, Philadelphia, PA: The Westminster Press.

Carr, David M. (1996) *Reading the Fractures of Genesis: Historical and Literary Approaches*, Louisville, KY: Westminster/John Knox Press.

Carter, Margaret L. (ed.) (1989) *The Vampire in Literature: A Critical Bibliography*, Ann Arbor, MI: University of Michigan Research Press.

Casey, Edward S. (1993) *Getting Back into Place: Toward a Renewed Understanding of the Place-World*, Studies in Continental Thought, Bloomington, IN: Indiana University Press.

Charlesworth, James H. (1983) *The Old Testament Pseudepigrapha: Vol. I: Apocalyptic Literature and Testaments*, Garden City, NY: Doubleday.

Chow, Rey (1993) "Listening Otherwise, Music Miniaturized: A Different Type of Question About Revolution," in Simon During (ed.), *The Cultural Studies Reader*, London and New York: Routledge, 382–99.

Clines, David (1979) "The Significance of the 'Sons of God' Episode (Genesis 6: 1–4) in the Context of the 'Primeval History' (Genesis 1–11)," *Journal for the Study of the Old Testament*, 13, 33–46.

—— (1994) "Theme in Genesis 1–11," in R.S. Hess and D.T. Tsumura (eds) *"I Studied Inscriptions from before the Flood": Ancient Near Eastern, Literary, and Linguistic Approaches to Genesis 1–11*, Winona Lake, MN: Eisenbrauns.

Cohn-Sherbok, Dan (1992) "Nephilim," *The Blackwell Dictionary of Judaica*, Oxford: Blackwell.

Coleridge, Samuel Taylor (1920) *Biographia Literaria*, Cambridge: Cambridge University Press

Confessions d'un Barjo (1992) J. Boivin (dir.) Centre Européen Cinématographique Rhone-Alpes.

Cooke, G. A. (1936) *A Critical and Exegetical Commentary on the Book of Ezekiel*, The International Critical Commentary, Edinburgh: T. & T. Clark.

Creed, Barbara (1993) *The Monstrous-Feminine: Film, Feminism, Psychoanalysis*, New York: Routledge.

Csikszentmihaly, Mihaly (1993) *The Evolving Self: A Psychology for the Third Millennium*, New York: HarperCollins.

Cullmann, Oskar (1978) *Early Christian Worship*, Philadelphia, PA: Westminster Press.

Curtis, James M. (1984) "Toward a Sociotechnological Interpretation of Popular Music in the Electronic Age," *Technology and Culture*, 25 (January), 91–102.

Davidson, Gustav (1967) *A Dictionary of Angels Including the Fallen Angels*, New York: The Free Press.

Davies, Chris Lawe (1993) "Aboriginal Rock Music: Space and Place," in Tony Bennett, *et al.* (eds) *Rock and Popular Music: Politics, Policies, Institutions*, Culture: Policies and Politics, London and New York: Routledge, 249–65.

Davies, Philip R. (1993) "Women, Men, Gods, Sex and Power: The Birth of a Biblical Myth," in Athalya Brenner (ed.) *A Feminist Companion to Genesis*, Sheffield: Sheffield Academic Press.

DeCurtis, Anthony (1991) "Introduction: The Sanctioned Power of Rock and Roll," *South Atlantic Quarterly*, 90 (Fall), in Anthony DeCurtis (ed.) *Rock and Roll and Culture*, Durham, NC: Duke University Press.

de Man, Paul (1979) *Allegories of Reading*, New Haven, CT: Yale University Press.

Desjardins, Michel (1990) *Sin in Valentinianism*, Atlanta, GA: Scholars Press.

Detwiler, Robert and Doty, William, G. (eds) (1990) *The Daemonic Imagination: Biblical Text and Secular Story*, Studies in Religion 60, Atlanta, GA: Scholars Press.

Dick, A.R. (1995) *Search for Philip K. Dick, 1928–1982: A Memoir and Biography of the Science Fiction Writing*, Lewiston, NY: Edwin Mellen Press.

Dick, Philip K. (1953) "Second Variety," *Space Science Fiction*.

—— (1962) *The Man in the High Castle*, New York: Putnam.

—— (1966) "We Can Remember it for you Wholesale," *Magazine of Fantasy and Science Fiction*.

—— (1968) *Do Androids Dream of Electric Sheep?*, Garden City, NY: Doubleday.

—— (1975) *Confessions of a Crap Artist*, New York: Entwhistle Books.

—— (1977) *A Scanner Darkly*, New York: DAW Books.

—— (with R. Zelazny) (1976) *Deus Irae*, Garden City, NY: Doubleday.

—— (1978) "Si vous trouvez ce monde mauvais, vous devriez en voir quelques autres," in J. Goimard (ed.) *L'Année 1977–78 de la S.F. et du fantastique*, Paris: Julliard.

—— (1981a) *The Divine Invasion*, New York: Timescape.

—— (1981b) *VALIS*, New York: Bantam.

—— (1982) *The Transmigration of Timothy Archer*, New York: Timescape.

—— (1985) *Radio Free Albemuth*, New York: Arbor House.

—— (1986) "How to Build a Universe that Doesn't Fall Apart Two Days Later?," in *P.K. Dick I Hope I Shall Arrive Soon*, New York: Doubleday.

—— (1987) "Was Horselover Fat a Flake?," *The Philip K. Dick Society Newsletter*, 15, 5–6.

Dodd, C.H. (1978) *The Parables of the Kingdom*, London: Fount Paperbacks.

Doty, Gene (1980) *Fishing at Easter* (with *Break in the Winter* by Elias Chiasson), *BkMk Poets 80–81*, BkMk Press, Kansas City, MO.

—— (1981) *Geometries of Light*, Wheaton, IL: Harold Shaw Publishers.

—— (1996) "Inverse Oracle," *THOTH*, Online E-Zine (30 September).

Doty, William G. (1986a) "Infinite Games of Purified Similitude," *Art Papers*, 6/2, 41–3.

—— (1986b) *Mythography: The Study of Myths and Rituals*, Tuscaloosa, AL: University of Alabama Press.

—— (1988) "The Heterogeneous Other and the Examined Life," *Soundings: An Interdisciplinary Journal*, 71/1, 155–69

—— (1990) "Writing the Blurred Genres of Postmodern Ethnography," *Annals of Scholarship: Studies of the Humanities and Social Sciences*, 6/2 and 3, 267–87.

—— (1991) "Exploring the Grammar of Apokalypse: Ballard's *The Atrocity Exhibition*," *Art Papers*, 15/6, 34–6.

—— (1992) "J.G. Ballard: Contemporary Apocalyptic Spirituality," *Continuum: A Journal of History, Hermeneutics, and Social Concern*, 2/1, 30–42

—— (1993) *Myths of Masculinity*, New York: Crossroad.

—— (1996) "Baring the Flesh: Contemporary Masculine Iconography," in Björn Krondorfer (ed.) *Men's Bodies, Men's God: Male Identities in a (Post) Christian Culture*, New York: New York University Press; 267–308.

—— (forthcoming) "Sweet Machines, Hard Bodies, and Soft Porn: Images in the Social Construction of Gender," *Mattoid* (Australia).

Douglas, Mary (1970) *Natural Symbols: Explorations in Cosmology*, New York: Pantheon.

Drower, E.S. (1956) *Water into Wine*, London: Murray.

Drury, John (1976) *Tradition and Design in Luke's Gospel*, Atlanta, GA: John Knox Press.

Dumont, J.-N. (1988) "Between Faith and Melancholy: Irony and the Gnostic Meaning of Dick's 'Divine Trilogy,'" *Science-Fiction Studies*, 15, 251–3.

Dutton, Kenneth R. (1995) *The Perfectible Body: The Western Ideal of Male Physical Development*, New York: Continuum.

Dyer, Richard (1990) "In Defense of Disco," in Simon Frith and Andrew Goodwin (eds) *On Record: Rock, Pop, and the Written Word*, London: Routledge, 410–18.

Eddins, Dwight (1984) "Orphic contra Gnostic: Religious Conflict in *Gravity's Rainbow*," *Modern Language Quarterly*, 45/2, 163–90.

—— (1990) *The Gnostic Pynchon*, Bloomington, IN: Indiana University Press.

Eichrodt, Walther (1970) *Ezekiel: A Commentary*, Old Testament Library, London: SCM.

Eilberg-Schwartz, Howard and Doniger, Wendy (eds) (1995) *Off with Her Head: The Denial of Women's Identity in Myth, Religion, and Culture*, Berkeley, CA: University of California Press.

Eliade, Mircea (1959) *The Sacred and the Profane*, trans. W. Trask, New York: Harcourt Brace Jovanovich.

—— (1977) *No Souvenirs: Journal 1957–1969*, trans. F. H. Johnson, Jr, New York: Harper & Row.

Encyclopedia of Religion and Ethics (1908–26), ed. J. Hastings, New York: Scribner's.

The Englishman's Greek New Testament (n.d.) London: Bagster & Sons.

Eslinger, Lyle (1979) "A Contextual Identification of the *bene ha'elohim* and *benoth ha'adam* in Genesis 6: 1–4," *Journal for the Study of the Old Testament*, 13, 65–73.

Fenton, J.C. (1963) *Saint Matthew*, Baltimore, MD: Penguin Books.

Finch, Sheila (1986) *Triad*, New York: Bantam.

Fitting, P. (1987) "Futurecop: The Neutralization of Revolt in *Blade Runner*," *Science Fiction Studies*, 14, 340–54.

Flanagan, Bill (1992) "Shadow Boxing with Axl Rose," interview in *Musician* (June), http://www.students.uiuc.edu/-gray/music92.html.

Foucault, Michel (1986) *The Care of the Self*, trans. Robert Gurley, *The History of Sexuality*, vol. 3, New York: Pantheon.

Fourier, Charles (1971) *The Utopian Vision of Charles Fourier*, ed. Jonathan Beecher and Richard Bienvenu, Boston, MA: Beacon.

Frank, Janrae, Stine, Jean and Forrest J. Ackerman (eds) (1994) *New Eves: Science Fiction about the Extraordinary Women of Today and Tomorrow*, Stamford, CT: Longmeadow Press.

Frazer, Sir James George (1922) *The Golden Bough: A Study in Magic and Religion*, New York: Macmillan, 1969.

Freedman, C. (1988) "Editorial Introduction," *Science-Fiction Studies*, 15, 121–30.

Freedman, H. and Maurice Simon (trans. and ed.) (1939) *Midrash Rabbah: Genesis I*, London: The Soncino Press.

Freud, Sigmund (1938) *The Interpretation of Dreams*, trans and ed. A. A. Brill, in *The Basic Writings of Sigmund Freud*, New York: Modern Library.

—— (1950) *Totem and Taboo*, trans. James Strachey, New York: W.W. Norton.

—— (1955) "The 'Uncanny,'" trans. Alix Strachey, in *Complete Psychological Works*, vol. 17, 219–56. London: Hogarth Press.

Frith, Simon (1981) "'The Magic That Can Set You Free': The Ideology of Folk and the Myth of the Rock Community," *Popular Music*, 1, 159–68.

—— (1990) "Afterthoughts," in Simon Frith and Andrew Goodwin (eds) *On Record: Rock, Pop, and the Written Word*, London: Routledge, 419–24.

Frith, Simon and McRobbie, Angela (1990) "Rock and Sexuality," in Simon Frith and Andrew Goodwin (eds) *On Record: Rock, Pop, and the Written Word*, London: Routledge, 371–89.

Fuller, R. Buckminster (1981) *Critical Path*, New York: St Martin's.

Gablik, Suzi (1995) *Conversations Before the End of Time*, New York: Thames & Hudson.

Galbreath, R. (1982) "Salvation-Knowledge: Ironic Gnosticism in *VALIS* and *The Flight to Lucifer*," in G. Wolfe (ed.) *Science Fiction Dialogues*, Chicago, IL: Academy.

—— (1983) "Redemption and Doubt in Philip K. Dick's VALIS Trilogy," *Extrapolation*, 24, 105–15.

Garofalo, Reebee (1993) "Black Popular Music: Crossing Over or Going Under?," in Tony Bennett, *et al.* (eds) *Rock and Popular Music: Politics, Policies, Institutions*, Culture: Policies and Politics, London and New York: Routledge, 231–48.

Garratt, Sheryl (1990) "Teenage Dreams," in Simon Frith and Andrew Goodwin (eds) *On Record: Rock, Pop, and the Written Word*, London: Routledge, 399–409.

Gay, David (1995) "Milton's Samson and the Figure of the Old Testament Giant," *Literature and Theology*, 9, 4, 355–69.

Gearhart, Sally J. (1991) "The Myth of the Matriarchy: Annulling Patriarchy Through the Regeneration of Time," *Communication Studies*, 42/4, 371–82.

Geertz, C. (1973) *The Interpretation of Cultures*, New York: Basic Books.

Gendron, Bernard (1986) "Theodor Adorno Meets the Cadillacs," in Tania Modleski (ed.) *Studies in Entertainment: Critical Approaches to Mass Culture*, foreword Kathleen Woodward, Theories of Contemporary Culture 7, Bloomington, IN: Indiana University Press, 18–36.

Gesenius (1829–32 [1964]) *Hebrew and Chaldee Lexicon to the Old Testament Scriptures*, trans. Samuel Prideaux Tregelles, Grand Rapids, MI: Wm. B. Eerdmans.

Ginzberg, Louis (1968) *Legends of the Jews: Vol. 1: Biblical Times and Characters from the Creation Jacob*, Philadelphia, PA: The Jewish Publication Society of America.

Girling, John (1993) *Myths and Politics in Western Societies: Evaluating the Crisis of Modernity in the United States, Germany, and Great Britain*, New Brunswick, NJ: Transaction.

Gottlieb, Roger S. (ed.) (1996) *This Sacred Earth: Religion, Nature, Environment*, New York: Routledge.

Gramsci, Antonio (1971) *Selections from the Prison Notebooks*, Quentin Hoare and Nowell Smith (eds), London: Lawrence & Wishart.

Graves, Robert and Raphael Patai (1963) *Hebrew Myths: The Book of Genesis*, London: Cassell.

Greenberg, Moshe (1983) *Ezekiel 1–20: A New Translation with Introduction and Commentary*, The Anchor Bible, vol. 22, Garden City, NY: Doubleday.

Grimm, Jacob Ludwig and Wilhelm Karl (1812–22) *Household Stories from the Collection of the Brothers Grimm*, trans. Lucy Crane, New York: Dover.

Grossberg, Lawrence (1984) "Another Boring Day in Paradise: Rock and Roll and the Empowerment of Everyday Life," *Popular Music*, 4, 225–58.

—— (1990) "Is There Rock After Punk?," in Simon Frith and Andrew Goodwin (eds) *On Record: Rock, Pop, and the Written Word*, London: Routledge, 111–23.

—— (1993) "The Framing of Rock: Rock and the New Conservatism," *Rock and Popular Music: Politics, Policies, Institutions*, Tony Bennett *et al.* (eds), London and New York: Routledge.

Guns n' Roses (1987) *Appetite for Destruction*, Compact Disk, producer Mike Clink, David Geffen Records, MCA, Universal City, CA.

—— (1988) *G n' R Lies*, Compact Disk, producer Guns n' Roses and Mike Clink, David Geffen Records, MCA, Universal City, CA.

—— (1991) *Use Your Illusion*, Compact Disk, producer Mike Clink, vols 1–2, David Geffen Records, MCA, Universal City, CA; citations from *The Garden, Garden of Eden, Get in the Ring*.

Hackett, N. (1988) "Letter," *The Philip K. Dick Society Newsletter* 16: 4.

Halperin, D.A. (1983) "Gnosticism in High Tech: Science Fiction and Cult Formation," in D. Halperin (ed.) *Psychodynamic Perspectives on Religion, Sect and Cult*, Boston, MA: John Wright.

Hart, Clive and Stevenson, Kay Gilliland (1995) *Heaven and the Flesh: Imagery of Desire from the Renaissance to the Rococo*, New York: Cambridge University Press.

Hassan, Ihab (1975) *Paracriticisms: Seven Speculations of the Times*, Urbana, IL: University of Illinois Press.

Hawthorne, Nathaniel (1966) *Selected Stories of Nathaniel Hawthorne*, Alfred Kazin (ed.), New York: Fawcett.

Hawthorne, Susan and Klein, Renate (eds) (1991) *Angels of Power and Other Reproductive Creations*, Melbourne: Sinifex Press.

Healy, Raymond J. and McComas, J. Francis (eds) (1975) *Adventures in Time and Space: An Anthology of Science Fiction Stories*, New York: Ballantine; first published, 1946.

Heilbroner, Robert L. (1974) *An Inquiry into the Human Prospect: Updated and Reconsidered for the 1980s*, New York: W.W. Norton; 2nd edn, 1988.

Hendel, Ronald S. (1987a) "When the Sons of God Cavorted with the Daughters of Men," *Bible Review* (Summer), 8–13, 37.

—— (1987b) "Of Demigods and the Deluge: Toward an Interpretation of Genesis 6: 1–4," *Journal of Biblical Literature*, 106, 1 (March), 13–26.

—— (1993) "Nephilim," in Bruce M. Metzger and Michael D. Coogan (eds) *The Oxford Companion to the Bible*, New York: Oxford University Press.

Herman, Andrew (1992) *Postmodern Culture* 4/1 (September) (World Wide Web page), http: //jefferson.village.virginia.edu/pmc.contents.all.html.

—— (1993) "Review of Andrew Goodwin," *Dancing in the Distraction Factory: Music Television and Popular Culture*, Minneapolis, MN: University of Minnesota Press.

Hill, Trent (1991) "The Enemy Within: Censorship in Rock Music in the 1950s," *South Atlantic Quarterly*, 90 (Fall), 675–708, in Anthony DeCurtis (ed.) *Rock and Roll and Culture*, Durham, NC: Duke University Press.

Hillman, James (1979) *The Dream and the Underworld*, New York: Harper-Collins.

Hinds, Elizabeth Jane Wall (1992) "The Devil Sings the *Blues*: Heavy Metal, Gothic *Fiction* and 'Postmodern' Discourse," *Journal of Popular Culture*, 26 (Winter), 151–64.

Hirsch, Emil G. (1916) "Fall of Angels," in Isidore Singer (ed.) *The Jewish Encyclopedia*, New York: Funk & Wagnalls.

Hoeller, S.A. (1982) *The Gnostic Jung and the Seven Sermons to the Dead*, Wheaton, IL: The Theosophical Publishing House.

Hong, Joseph (1989) "Problems in an Obscure Passage: Notes on Genesis 6.1–4," *The Bible Translator*, 40, 2, 419–26.

Howe, Deborah and James (1979) *Bunnicula,* New York: Avon.

Hume, Kathryn (1984) *Fantasy and Mimesis: Responses to Reality in Western Literature*, New York: Methuen.

Huntington, John (1982) *The Logic of Fantasy: H.G. Wells and Science Fiction*, New York: Columbia University Press.

Ingebretsen, Edward J. (1996) *Maps of Heaven, Maps of Hell: Religious Terror as Memory from the Puritans to Stephen King*, Armonk, NY: M.E. Sharpe.

Isaac, E. (trans.) (1983) "1 Enoch," in James Charlesworth (ed.) *The Old Testament Pseudipigrapha: Vol. 1: Apocalyptic Literature and Testaments*, Garden City, NY: Doubleday.

Jackson, Rosemary (1981) *Fantasy: The Literature of Subversion*, London: Methuen.

—— (1988) *Fantasy: The Literature of Subversion*, New Accents, London and New York: Routledge.

Jakobson, Roman (1987) *Language and Literature*, Krystyna Pomorska and Stephen Rudy (eds) Cambridge, MA: Belknap Press of Harvard University.

James, Dell (1989) "Interview with Axl Rose," *Rolling Stone*, 558 (August 10) (World Wide Web page), http: //www.students.uiuc.edu/7Etgray/axlrs89.html.

Jeremias, Joachim (1958) *The Parables of Jesus*, London: SCM.

Joll, James (1979) *The Anarchists*, 2nd edn, London: Methuen.

Jonas, Hans (1963) *The Gnostic Religion: The Message of the Alien God and the Beginnings of Christianity*, Boston, MA: Beacon.

Josephus (1980) *The Works of Flavius Josephus: Vol. 1: Antiquities of the Jews*, trans. William Whiston, Grand Rapids, MI: Baker Book House.

Keen, Sam (1986) *Faces of the Enemy: Reflections of the Hostile Imagination*, San Francisco, CA: Harper & Row.

Kenny, Glenn (1997) "David Cronenberg," *Premiere*, The Filmmaker Series (April), 67–70.

Kerman, J.B. (1991) *Retrofitting Blade Runner: Issues in Ridley Scott's Blade Runner and Philip K. Dick's Do Androids Dream of Electric Sheep?*, Bowling Green, OH: Bowling Green State University Popular Press.

Ketterer, David (1987) *Imprisoned in a Tesseract: The Life and Work of James Blish*, Kent, OH and London: Kent State University Press.

Kilmer, Anne Draffkorn (1987) "The Mesopotamian Counterparts of the Biblical Nephilim," in Edgar W. Conrad and Edward G. Newing (eds) *Perspectives on Language and Text*, Winona Lake, MN: Eisenbrauns.

King, K. (ed.) (1988) *Images of the Feminine in Gnosticism*, Philadelphia, PA: Fortress Press.

Kinney, J. (1985) "The Mysterious Revelations of Philip K. Dick," *Gnosis*, 1, 6–15.

Kinser, Bill, and Kleinman, Neil (1969) *The Dream That Was No More a Dream: A Search for Aesthetic Reality in Germany, 1890–1945*, New York: Harper.

Klassen, W. (1996) *Judas. Betrayer or Friend of Jesus?*, Minneapolis, MN: Fortress.

Klauck, H.-J. (1987) *Judas, ein Jünger des Herrn*, Freiburg: Herder.

Kloppenborg, John S. (1987) *The Formation of Q*, Institute for Antiquity and Christianity, Philadelphia, PA: Fortress Press.

—— (1988) *Q Parallels*, Sonoma, CA: Polebridge Press.

Krafft-Ebing, Richard von (1965) *Psychopathia Sexualis*, trans. Franklin S. Klaf, New York: Bell.

Kropotkin, Peter (1902) *Mutual Aid*, Harmondsworth: Penguin, 1939.

Lattimore, Richmond (trans.) (1979) *The Four Gospels and the Revelation*, New York: Dorset Press.

Leach, Edmund R. (1961) "Lévi-Strauss in the Garden of Eden: An Examination of Some Recent Developments in the Analysis of Myth," in

Transactions of the New York Academy of Sciences, series 2, vol. 23, 4, 386–96.

Led Zeppelin (1968) *Led Zeppelin I*, Atlantic Recording Corporation, New York.

Lévi-Strauss, Claude (1967) *Structural Anthropology*, trans. Claire Jacobson and Brooke Grundfest Schoepf, New York: Anchor.

Lewis, C.S. (1965a) *The Abolition of Man, or Reflections on Education with Special Reference to the Teaching of English in the Upper Forms of Schools*, New York: Macmillan.

—— (1965b) *That Hideous Strength*, New York: Macmillan.

—— (1982) *On Stories and Other Essays on Literature*, Walter Hooper (ed.), New York: Harcourt Brace Jovanovich.

Light, Alan (1991) "About a Salary or Reality?—Rap's Recurrent Conflict," *South Atlantic Quarterly*, 90 (Fall) , 85–70, in Anthony DeCurtis (ed.) *Rock and Roll and Culture*, Durham, NC: Duke University Press.

Limbeck, M. (1976) "Das Judasbild im Neuen Testament aus christlicher Sicht," in H.L. Goldschmidt and M. Limbeck (eds) *Heilvoller Verrat? Judas im Neuen Testament*, Stuttgart: Katholisches Bibelwerk.

Link, Luther (1995) *The Devil: The Archfiend in Art from the Sixth to the Sixteenth Century*, New York: Harry N. Abrams.

Linton, Ralph (1936) *The Study of Man*, Indianapolis, IN: Appleton-Century-Crofts.

Lippard, Lucy R. (1983) *Overlay: Contemporary Art and the Art of Prehistory*, New York: Pantheon.

—— (1990) *Mixed Blessings: New Art in a Multicultural America*, New York: Pantheon.

Llosa, Mario Vargas (1993) *The Storyteller*, New York: Penguin.

Lorenz, Konrad (1966) *On Aggression*, trans. Marjorie Kerr Wilson, New York: Harcourt Brace Jovanovich.

Lucretius (1965) *The Nature of the Universe*, trans. Ronald Latham, Baltimore, MD: Penguin Classics.

Lüthi, Max (1970) *Once Upon a Time: On the Nature of Fairy Tales*, trans. Lee Chadeayne and Paul Gottwald, New York: Frederick Ungar.

Machover, T. (1987) "VALIS: The Opera," *The Philip K. Dick Society Newsletter*, 15, 1–3.

MacKay, D.A. (1984) "Science Fiction and Gnosticism," *The Missouri Review* 7: 112–19.

—— (1988) *Philip K. Dick*, Boston, MA: Twayne.

MacLeish, Archibald (1957) *"J.B.": A Play in Verse*, New York: Houghton Mifflin.

Malmgren, C.D. (1980) "Philip Dick's *Man in the High Castle* and the Nature of Science-Fictional Worlds," in G.E. Slusser, G.R. Guffey and M. Rose (eds) *Bridges to Science Fiction*, Carbondale, IL: Southern Illinois University Press.

Manlove, C.N. (1975) *Modern Fantasy: Five Studies*, Cambridge: Cambridge University Press.

—— (1992a) "The Bible in Fantasy," in *Semeia 60: Fantasy and the Bible*, George Aichele and Tina Pippin (eds), Atlanta, GA: Scholars Press.

—— (1992b) *Christian Fantasy: from Twelve Hundred to the Present*. South Bend, OH: University of Notre Dame Press.

Marshall, Peter (1993) *Demanding the Impossible: A History of Anarchism*, London: Fontana.

Martin, Dale (1995) "Heterosexism and the Interpretation of Romans 1: 18–32," *Biblical Interpretation*, 3, 3, 332–55.

Mauss, M. (1967) *The Gift*, trans. I. Cunnison, New York: W.W. Norton.

Merkur, D. (1993) *Gnosis: An Esoteric Tradition of Mystical Visions and Unions*, Albany, NY: State University of New York Press.

Milton, John (1667–74) *Paradise Lost*, Merritt Y. Hughes (ed.) New York: Odyssey, 1962.

Miles, Jack (1995) *God: A Biography*, New York: Alfred A. Knopf.

Miller, H. G. (1990) "Angel Scare," *Saturday Evening Post* (September), 88–9, 97.

Morrow, James (1996) "Bible Stories for Adults, no. 17: The Deluge," *Bible Stories for Adults*, New York: Harcourt Brace Jovanovich.

Neely, Kim (1992) "Interview with Axl Rose," *Rolling Stone* (2 April) (World Wide Web page), http://www.students.uiuc.edu/7Et-gray/axlrs92.html.

Newman, Robert C. (1984) "The Ancient Exegesis of Genesis 6: 2, 4," *Grace Theological Journal*, 5, 1, 13–36.

The New Oxford Annotated Bible with the Apocrypha (1977), H. G. May and Bruce Metzger (eds), New York: Oxford University Press.

The New Testament in Syriac (1966), London: the British and Foreign Bible Society.

Niditch, Susan (1985) *Chaos to Cosmos: Studies in Biblical Patterns of Creation*, Chico, CA: Scholars Press.

Nineham, D.E. (1963) *Saint Mark*, Harmondsworth: Penguin Books.

Noel, Daniel C. (1986) *Approaching Earth: A Search for the Mythic Significance of the Space Age*, Warwick, NY: Amity House.

—— (1997) *The Soul of Shamanism: Western Fantasies, Imaginal Realities*, New York: Continuum.

O'Connor, Francis V. (1980) "The Usable Future: The Role of Fantasy in the Promotion of a Consumer Society for Art," in Helen A. Harrison *et al.*, *Dawn of a New Day: The New York World's Fair, 1939/40*, New York: New York University Press.

Oduyoye, Modupe (1984) *The Sons of the Gods and the Daughters of Men: An Afro-Asiatic Interpretation of Genesis 1–11*, Maryknoll, PA: Orbis Books.

Olander, J. and Greenberg, M. (eds) (1983) *Philip K. Dick*, New York: Taplinger.

Otto, Rudolf (1958) *The Idea of the Holy: An Inquiry into the Non-rational Factor in the Idea of the Divine and Its Relation to the Rational*, trans. J. W. Harvey, London and New York: Oxford University Press.

Otto, W.F. (1965) *Dionysus*, Bloomington, IN: Indiana University Press.

Overholt, Thomas W. (1986) *Prophecy in Cross-cultural Perspective: A Sourcebook for Biblical Researchers*, Society of Biblical Literature Sources for Biblical Study, vol. 17, Atlanta, GA: Scholars Press.

—— (1989) *Channels of Prophecy: The Social Dynamics of Prophetic Activity*, Minneapolis, MN: Fortress.

Oxford English Dictionary (1971), Compact Edition, New York: Oxford University Press.

Pagels, Elaine (1979) *The Gnostic Gospels*, New York: Vintage.

—— (1995) *The Origin of Satan*. New York: Random House.

Palmer, Robert (1991) "The Church of the Sonic Guitar," in Anthony DeCurtis (ed.) *Rock and Roll and Culture*, Durham, NC: Duke University Press, 649–73.

Parker, Simon B. (1978) "Possession Trance and Prophecy in Post-exilic Israel," *Vetus Testamentum*, 28 (July), 271–85.

Pearson, Carol (1986) *The Hero Within: Six Archetypes We Live By*, San Francisco, CA: Harper & Row.

Pearson, Carol, and Pope, Katherine (1981) *The Female Hero in American and British Literature*, New York: Bowker.

Peretti, Frank E. (1986) *This Present Darkness*, Westchester, IL: Crossway Books.

Petersen, David L. (1979) "Genesis 6: 1–4, Yahweh and the Organization of the Cosmos," *Journal for the Study of the Old Testament*, 13, 47–64.

Peterson, Richard and Berger, David G. (1990) "Circles in Symbol Production: the Case of Popular Music," in Simon Frith and Andrew Goodwin (eds) *On Record: Rock, Pop, and the Written Word*, London: Routledge, 140–59.

Plank, Robert (1968) *The Emotional Significance of Imaginary Beings*, Springfield, IL: Chas C. Thomas.

Platt, C. (1980) *The Dream Makers*, New York: Berkley.

Proudhon, Pierre-Joseph (1876) *What is Property?*, trans. Benjamin Tucker, New York: Dover, 1970.

Rabkin, Eric S. (1976) *The Fantastic in Literature*, Princeton, NJ: Princeton University Press.

—— (1979) *Fantastic Worlds: Myths, Tales, and Stories*, New York: Oxford University Press.

—— (1980) "Fairy Tales and Science Fiction," in George E. Slusser, George R. Guffey, and Mark Rose (eds) *Bridges to Science Fiction*, Carbondale, IL: Southern Illinois University Press.

Rabkin, Eric S., Slusser, George and Westfahl, Gary (1996) *Foods of the Gods: Eating and the Eaten in Fantasy and Science Fiction*, Athens, GA: University of Georgia Press.

Rashkow, Ilona, N. (1993) *The Phallacy of Genesis: A Feminist-Psychoanalytic Approach*, Louisville, KY: Westminster/John Knox Press.

Regev, Motti (1994) "Producing Artistic Value: The Case of Rock Music," *The Sociological Quarterly*, 35 (February), 85–102.

Reps, P. (1961) *Zen Flesh, Zen Bones*, New York: Anchor Books.

Roberts, Robin (1993) *A New Species: Gender and Science in Science Fiction*, Urbana, IL: University of Illinois Press, 2nd edn.

Robinson, Kim Stanley (1992) *Red Mars*, London: HarperCollins Publishers.

—— (1993) *Green Mars*, London: HarperCollins Publishers.

—— (1996) *Blue Mars*, London: HarperCollins Publishers.

Robinson, James M. (ed.) (1977) *The Nag Hammadi Library in English*, 2nd edn, New York: Harper.

—— (ed.) (1988) *The Nag Hammadi Library in English*, 3rd edn, Leiden: E.J. Brill.

Rose, Axl (1992a) "Interview by *Interview Magazine*," (WorldWide Web page), http: //www.students.uiuc.edu/7Et-gray/axlint.html.

—— (1992b) "Interview by *Rip Magazine*," (World Wide Web page), http: //www.students.uiuc.edu/7Et-gray/axlrip92.html.

Roth, Joseph (1930) *Job: The Story of a Simple Man*, New York: Viking, 1985.

Rubey, Dan (1991) "Voguing at the Carnival: Desire and Pleasure on MTV," *The South Atlantic Quarterly*, 90 (Fall), 871–906, in Anthony DeCurtis (ed.) *Rock and Roll and Culture*, Durham, NC: Duke University Press.

Rudolph, Kurt (1983) *Gnosis: The Nature and History of Gnosticism*, trans. and ed. Robert McLachlan Wilson, San Francisco, CA: Harper & Row; first published in German, 1977.

Russ, Joanna (1972) "The Image of Women in Science Fiction," in Susan Koppelman Cornillon (ed.) *Images of Women in Fiction: Feminist Perspectives*, Bowling Green, OH: Bowling Green University Popular Press.

Russell, Jeffrey Burton (1981) *Satan: The Early Christian Tradition*, Ithaca, NY and London: Cornell University Press.

Sammon, P.M. (1993) "Do Androids Dream of Unicorns? The Seven Faces of *Blade Runner*," *Video Watchdog*, 20, 32–59.

—— (1996) *Future Noir: The Making of Blade Runner*, New York: Harper-Collins.

Screamers (1995) C. Duguay (dir.) Triumph Films, Culver City, CA.

Sarna, Nahum M. (1989) *The JPS Torah Commentary: Genesis*, Philadelphia, PA: The Jewish Publication Society.

Schaberg, Jane (1987) *The Illegitimacy of Jesus: A Feminist Theological Interpretation of the Infancy Narratives*, San Francisco, CA: Harper & Row.

Scherman, Nosson (1993) *The Chumash. The Torah: Haftaros and Five Megillos with a Commentary Anthologized from Rabbinic Writings*, The Stone Edition, Brooklyn, NY: Mesorah Publications.

Schlobin, Roger C. (1988) "Children of a Darker God: A Taxonomy of Deep Horror Fiction and Film and their Mass Popularity," *Journal of the Fantastic in the Arts*, 1, 1, 25–50.

Schmidt, C. (1962) *Koptisch-gnostische Schriften – Bd. 1: Die Pistis Sopia. Die beiden Bücher des Jeu. Unbekanntes altgnostisches Werk*, 3rd edn rev. E. Till, Berlin: Deutsche Akademie der Wissenschaften.

Schneider, Kirk J. (1993) *Horror and the Holy: Wisdom-Teachings of the Monster Tale*, Chicago, IL: Open Court.

Schusser, George (1987) "Sciences of the Mind in French Science Fiction," *Annals of Scholarship: Studies of the Humanities and Social Sciences*, 4/1, 95.

Schwarz, G. (1988) *Jesus und Judas: Aramaistische Untersuchungen zur Jesus-Judas-Überlieferung der Evangelien und der Apostelgeschichte*, Beitrage zur Wissenschaft vom Alten und Neuen Testament 123, Stuttgart: Kohlhammer.

Segal, R.A. (ed.) (1992) *The Gnostic Jung*, Princeton, NJ: Princeton University Press.

Service, Robert, W. (1907) "The Woman and the Angel," in *The Spell of the Yukon and Other Verses*, New York: Barse & Hopkins.

Shelley, Mary (1969) *Frankenstein, or The Modern Prometheus*, M.K. Joseph (ed.), New York: Oxford University Press.

Shiner, Lewis (1988) *Deserted Cities of the Heart*, New York: Bantam.

Shipley, Joseph T. (1984) *The Origins of English Words: A Discursive Dictionary of Indo-European Roots*, Baltimore, MD: Johns Hopkins University Press.

Shumway, David R. (1991) "Rock and Roll as a Cultural Practice," *South Atlantic Quarterly*, 90 (Fall), 753–70, in Anthony DeCurtis (ed.) *Rock and Roll and Culture*, Durham, NC: Duke University Press.

Simpson, D.P. (ed.) (1987) *Cassell's Latin and English Dictionary*, New York: Collier.

Singer, J. (1992) *A Gnostic Book of Hours: Keys to Inner Wisdom*, San Francisco, CA: HarperSanFrancisco.

Soleri, Paolo (1969) *Arcology: The City in the Image of Man*, Cambridge: MIT Press.

—— (1981) *The Omega Seed: An Eschatological Hypothesis*, Garden City, NY: Anchor/Doubleday.

Spivak, Gayatri Chakravorty (1983) "Displacement and the Discourse of Woman," in Mark Krupnick (ed.) *Displacement: Derrida and After*, Bloomington, IN: Indiana University Press.

Stableford, Brian M. (1979) *A Clash of Symbols: The Triumph of James Blish*, San Bernadino, CA: Borgo Press.

Stapleton, L. (ed.) (1960) *H. D. Thoreau: A Writer's Journal*, New York: Dover.

Stephens, Walter (1989) *Giants in Those Days: Folklore, Ancient History, and Nationalism*, Lincoln, NB: University of Nebraska Press.

Stewart, Susan (1984) *On Longing: Narratives of the Miniature, the Gigantic, the Souvenir, the Collection*, Baltimore, MD: Johns Hopkins University Press.

Stoler, Ann Laura (1995) *Race and the Education of Desire: Foucault's History of Sexuality and the Colonial Order of Things*, Durham, NC: Duke University Press.

Stratton, Jon (1983) "Capitalism and Romantic Ideology in the Record Business," *Popular Music*, 3, 143–56.

Straw, Will (1993) "Characterizing Rock Music Culture: The Case of Heavy Metal," in Simon During (ed.) *The Cultural Studies Reader*, London and New York: Routledge, 368–81.

Sturma, Michael (1992) "The Politics of Dancing: When Rock n' Roll Came to Australia," *Journal of Popular Culture*, 25 (Spring), 123–42.

Sutin, L. (1989) *Divine Invasions: A Life of Philip K. Dick*, New York: Harmony.

—— (ed.) (1991) *In Pursuit of VALIS: Selections from his Exegesis*, Novato: Underwood-Miller.

—— (ed.) (1995) *The Shifting Realities of Philip K. Dick: Selected Literary and Philosophical Writings*, New York: Pantheon.

Swift, Jonathan (1726) *Gulliver's Travels*, in Louis A. Landa (ed.) *Gulliver's Travels and Other Writings*, Boston, MA: Houghton Mifflin, 1960.

—— (1729) *A Modest Proposal*, London: Constable.

Tarlin, Jan (1997) "Utopia and Pornography in Ezekiel: Violence, Hope, and the Shattered Male Subject," in Timothy K. Beal and David M. Gunn (eds) *Reading Bibles, Writing Bodies: Identity and the Book*, Biblical Limits, London and New York: Routledge, 175–83.

Taylor, Vincent (1953) *The Gospel According to Saint Mark*, London: Macmillan.

They Might Be Giants (1990) *Flood*, Elektra Entertainment Group, Beverley Hills, CA.

Thompson, William I. (1981) *The Time Falling Bodies Take to Light: Mythology, Sexuality, and the Origins of Culture*, New York: St Martin's.

Tigunait, Pandit R. (1996) "Yoga Prophecies and the 21st Century," *Yoga International* (November), 24–31.

Todorov, Tzvetan (1973) *The Fantastic*, trans. Richard Howard, Cleveland, OH: Case Western Reserve University Press.

Tolkien, J.R.R. (1966) "On Fairy Stories," in *The Tolkien Reader*, New York: Ballantine Books, 33–99.

Total Recall (1990) P. Verhoeven (dir.) Columbia TriStar, Culver City, CA with Carolco International, NV.

Turner, Victor (1985) *On the Edge of the Bush: Anthropology as Experience*, Anthropology of Form and Meaning, Edith L.B. Turner (ed.), Tucson, AZ: University of Arizona Press.

Ullestad, Neal (1987) "Rock and Rebellion: Subversive Effects of Live Aid and 'Sun City,'" *Popular Music* 6 (January), 67–92.

Umland, S.J. (1995) "To Flee from Dionysus: *Enthousiasmos* from 'Upon the Dull Earth' to *VALIS*," in S.J. Umland (ed.) *Philip K. Dick: Contemporary Critical Interpretations*, Westport, CT: Greenwood Press.

van Gemeren, Willem A. (1981) "The Sons of God in Genesis 6: 1–4 (An Example of Evangelical Demythologization?)," *Westminster Theological Journal*, 43, 320–48.

von Franz, M. L. (1964) "The Process of Individuation," in *Man and His Symbols*, Carl G. Jung and M.-L. Von Franz (eds) London: Aldus Books.

von Rad, Gerhard (1972) *Genesis: A Commentary*, Philadelphia, PA: Westminster Press.

Waggoner, Lynda S. (1996) *Fallingwater: Frank Lloyd Wright's Romance with Nature*, New York: Universe/Rizzoli.

Warner, Marina (1994) *From the Beast to the Blonde: On Fairy Tales and their Tellers*, New York: Farrar, Straus & Giroux.

Warrick, P. (1985) "Philip K. Dick's Answers to Eternal Riddles," in R. Reilly (ed.) *The Transcendent Adventure: Studies of Religion in Science Fiction/Fantasy*, Westport, CT: Greenwood.

—— (1987) *Mind in Motion: The Fiction of Philip K. Dick*, Carbondale, IL: Southern Illinois University Press.

Wellhausen, Julius (1885) *Prolegomena to the History of Ancient Israel*, trans. J.S. Black and A. Menzies, Edinburgh: Adam & Charles Black.

Wells, H.G. (1904) *The Food of the Gods. Seven Science Fiction Novels of H. G. Wells*, New York: Dover, 1934.

Wertheim, Margaret (1996) "Lux interior: In the Light World of Osmose, Char Davies is Expanding the Frontiers of Virtual Reality," *21°C: Scanning the Future: A Magazine of Culture, Technology, and Science*, 4, 26–31.

Westermann, Claus (1967) *Basic Forms of Prophetic Speech*, Philadelphia, PA: Westminster.

White, Robert J. (1975) [Artemidoros] *The Interpretation of Dreams*, Park Ridge, NJ: Noyes.

Williams, P. (1986) *Only Apparently Real: The World of Philip K. Dick*, New York: Arbor House.

Wilson, Robert R. (1972) "An Interpretation of Ezekiel's Dumbness," *Vetus Testamentum*, 32 (January), 91–104.

—— (1979) "Prophecy and Ecstasy: A Reexamination," *Journal of Biblical Literature*, 98, 321–37.

—— (1980) *Prophecy and Society in Ancient Israel*, Philadelphia, PA: Fortress.

Wings of Desire (1988), Wim Wenders (dir.) starring Bruno Ganz, Solveig Dommartin, Curt Bois, Peter Falk, Otto Sander, Orion Home Video, Los Angeles, CA.

Wolfe, Tom (1979) *The Right Stuff*, New York: Farrer.

Wrede, Wilhelm (1907) "Judas Ischariot in der urchristlichen Überlieferung," in *Vorträge und Studien*, Tübingen: J. Mohr.

Xanthakou, Margarita (1988) *Cendrillon et les soeurs cannibales*, Paris: Éditions de l'École des Hautes Études en Sciences Sociales.

Zimmerli, Walther (1979) *Ezekiel 1: A Commentary on the Book of the Prophet Ezekiel, Chapter 1–24*, trans. Ronald E. Clements, Hermeneia: a Critical and Historical Commentary on the Bible, Philadelphia, PA: Fortress.

Zipes, Jack (1984) *Breaking the Magic Spell*, New York: Methuen.
—— (1987) *Don't Bet on the Prince: Contemporary Feminist Fairy Tales in North America and England*, New York: Routledge.
—— (1988) *Fairy Tales and the Art of Subversion: The Classical Genre for Children and the Process of Civilization*, New York: Methuen.
—— (1992) "The Messianic Power of Fantasy in the Bible," in *Semeia 60: Fantasy and the Bible*, George Aichele and Tina Pippin (eds), Atlanta, GA: Scholars Press.
Žižek, Slavoj (1994) *The Metastases of Enjoyment: Six Essays on Woman and Causality*. London and New York: Verso.

INDEX OF NAMES
AND TERMS

INDEX OF BIBLICAL
REFERENCES